Persecution in Missions

Other 9Marks Titles

Overview Books
Nine Marks of a Healthy Church, by Mark Dever
How to Build a Healthy Church, by Mark Dever and Paul Alexander
The Compelling Community, by Mark Dever and Jamie Dunlop
The Rule of Love, by Jonathan Leeman
No Shortcut to Success, by Matt Rhodes

The Building Healthy Churches Series
Conversion, by Michael Lawrence
Evangelism, by J. Mack Stiles
Church Membership, by Jonathan Leeman
Expositional Preaching, by David Helm
Discipling, by Mark Dever
Deacons, by Matt Smethurst
Additional titles available

The Church Questions Series
How Can I Find Someone to Disciple Me?
How Can Women Thrive in the Local Church?
How Can Our Church Find a Faithful Pastor?
How Can I Love Church Members with Different Politics?
Additional titles available

Titles for New Christians
What Is the Gospel?, by Greg Gilbert
Who Is Jesus?, by Greg Gilbert
Why Trust the Bible?, by Greg Gilbert
Am I Really a Christian?, by Mike McKinley

Healthy Church Study Guides are available on all nine marks.

To explore all 9Marks titles, visit 9Marks.org/bookstore.

"Persecution was used by God to forge the early church, and it continues as an ever-present reality in much of the world today. Rhodes is ideally equipped to handle this subject. His missionary credentials are impeccable, his love for the church is evident to all who know him, and he fearlessly calls out poor theology that manifests in missiology. May this work edify the church and encourage those pilgrims who walk on, longing for their true homeland."

Brooks Buser, President, Radius International

"Some books highlight the challenges of suffering and persecution, but few apply it to the missionary life. With the mind of a theologian, the heart of a pastor, and the experience of a missionary, Matt Rhodes thoughtfully addresses the opposition and hardship that so many missionaries face. While many are initially naive to the hazards of Great Commission service, this book will help missionaries and those who send them to think biblically and prepare wisely for persecution in the task of missions. This book is much needed for any missions training."

E. D. Burns, missionary in Southeast Asia; Professor, Asia Biblical Theological Seminary; Executive Director of Training and Development, ABWE

"If you're looking for a book that valorizes missions and romanticizes suffering, this isn't it. Instead, Matt Rhodes provides a realistic perspective on persecution that's both joyful and sobering. Yes, the Bible teaches that persecution is a path to reward. But it's also an evil to be avoided. And these twin truths have plenty of practical implications for missionaries and those they serve."

Elliot Clark, author, *Evangelism as Exiles* and *Mission Affirmed*

"In *Persecution in Missions,* Matt Rhodes has proven yet again that he possesses both biblical wisdom and practical application for missionaries and churches as they navigate the modern missions world. Each chapter is packed with helpful insights. If you were helped by Rhodes's *No Shortcut to Success* and its call for missionary preparation, I know that you'll be encouraged by this fantastic new resource."

Ryan Robertson, President, Reaching & Teaching International Ministries

"For many in the Western world, persecution is a faraway concept. For many of our brothers and sisters in the majority world, however, persecution is a daily possibility. And in the places most in need of the gospel, persecution is an almost inevitable experience for a new convert. In this book, Matt Rhodes offers us a thorough, biblical, compassionate, and challenging perspective on persecution for the gospel. His work highlights how what Scripture says about persecution should practically shape our discipleship, our missions, and our prayer to be more biblically attuned."

Matt Bennett, Associate Professor of Missions and Theology, Cedarville University; Director of Long Term Ministries, Reaching & Teaching International Ministries

Persecution in Missions

A Practical Theology

Matt Rhodes

Foreword by Joshua

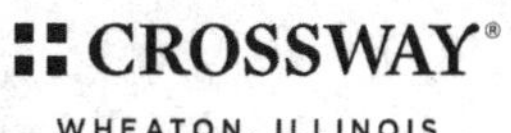

WHEATON, ILLINOIS

Persecution in Missions: A Practical Theology

Published by Crossway
1300 Crescent Street
Wheaton, Illinois 60187

Cover design: David Fassett

Cover image: Getty Images and Unsplash

First printing 2026

Printed in the United States of America

All emphases in Scripture quotations have been added by the author.

Trade paperback ISBN: 979-8-8749-0486-9
ePub ISBN: 979-8-8749-0488-3
PDF ISBN: 979-8-8749-0487-6

Library of Congress Cataloging-in-Publication Data

Names: Rhodes, Matt, 1979- author
Title: Persecution in missions: a practical theology / Matt Rhodes; foreword by Joshua.
Description: Wheaton, Illinois: Crossway, 2026 | Series: 9marks | Includes bibliographical references and index.
Identifiers: LCCN 2025013771 (print) | LCCN 2025013772 (ebook) | ISBN 9798874904869 (trade paperback) | ISBN 9798874904876 (pdf) | ISBN 9798874904883 (epub)
Subjects: LCSH: Missions
Classification: LCC BV2061.3 .R476 2026 (print) | LCC BV2061.3 (ebook) | DDC 266—dc23/eng/20250807
LC record available at https://lccn.loc.gov/2025013771
LC ebook record available at https://lccn.loc.gov/2025013772

Crossway is a publishing ministry of Good News Publishers.

BP 35 34 33 32 31 30 29 28 27 26
15 14 13 12 11 10 9 8 7 6 5 4 3 2 1

Contents

Foreword

MY ENGLISH-SPEAKING FRIENDS call me Joshua, but that is not my real name. In a Christian book about persecution and missions, I cannot use my real name. I live in a country where the proclamation of Christ is not only restricted but also viewed as a threat to national security. If I used my real name, then I would put myself and the people I serve and love in danger.

I grew up in an atheistic family. My grandfather held an important position in the local Communist Party, and my father was the head of the party at a university. According to their design for my life, I should not and could not have become a pastor. Yet by the grace of God, missionaries from across the ocean came into my life and introduced me to Jesus Christ. I think of S, who met me while playing basketball and asked me if I knew the true meaning of the Chinese character for "God." I think of D, who led me in studying the Bible once S left, even though I thought of him only as someone to practice language with and to bring me gifts from America. I think of C, who, even after I graduated from college, invited me to stay at his home in Nanjing. He and his wife took care of me as if they were my parents. The beautiful things these missionary friends did for me and other Chinese people are too numerous to count, yet I never understood how hard it was for them. I thought that since they come from a country far wealthier and freer than ours, and since they are missionaries, then they must be healthy and joyful Christians.

I assumed my Christian missionary friends had it easy until another missionary, M, showed me a text message from one of his fellow church members. This member was about to be disciplined by the church because of her serious, unrepented sin. M served as an elder in that church, and this church member warned M not to contact her anymore. She threatened M and said, "If you bring me up for church discipline, I will report you to law enforcement. Surely you don't want to be deported and have your decades of hard work go down the drain." M was clearly nervous. He knew he had to obey the Scriptures and lead the church faithfully, but he was worried about the consequences. He didn't want to jeopardize the fruit of many missionaries. He even started to wonder what he would do if he had to return to the United States. He had no savings and no alternative career plan.

Clearly, my perception was naive. Missionaries suffer too, and they sometimes suffer for doing the work of being a missionary.

Although many of these brothers and sisters have returned to the United States, I am still compelled to withhold their real names. They may never become household names among Christians, like Jim Elliot, but I'm grateful that the Lord knows their faithful labor and will reward them accordingly.

Unfortunately, I worry that many churches, when joyfully sending missionaries to the field, don't always prepare them for suffering and persecution. They might mention the possibility, but they don't prepare them sufficiently for the persecution they and their young disciples might endure.

That's why I'm so thankful for Matt Rhodes. He is solemn about what it means to suffer for missions not as a "necessary evil" but as a companion of joy in Christ. By developing a theology of missionary suffering, aspiring missionaries will be better equipped to mentor both other missionaries on the field and local Christians in restricted areas.

I'm glad I have the privilege of writing the foreword to this book. I have recommended and will continue to recommend it to aspiring Christian missionaries, coworkers in missions organizations, and elders in sending churches. Not only is the book rich in the theology of suffering, but it also applies that theology to real situations. The examples from the author's personal experience will help readers gain a more personal understanding of what suffering in missions looks like. I can tell you from personal experience that persecution in restricted areas is not limited to the forms described in this book, nor is this book a missionary's "crisis manual of persecution and suffering." Nonetheless, its theological framework places us face-to-face with the joy of Christ when persecution comes. After all, it was "for the joy that was set before him [that he] endured the cross, despising the shame" (Heb. 12:2).

May God use this book to equip missionaries, mission agencies, and sending churches to make the "surprises" of missions part of the joy. Take up this book so that you might suffer more joyfully.

Joshua (adopted English name)
PASTOR OF A HOUSE CHURCH IN CHINA

1

Separateness, Suffering, and Joy

For now we are pilgrims, we sigh, we groan.

AUGUSTINE
Exposition on Psalm 149

FATIME IS THE ONLY ONE LEFT NOW.

She doesn't know her age exactly, but she claims she's close to eighty. Four of her five children are dead. She's almost completely blind and stares out at the world through dull, barely open eyes. She has lost some of her fingers and toes to leprosy.

If you were to meet Fatime, though, the first thing you would notice is her joy. She sings to Jesus every day, which her Muslim neighbors have finally accepted. Years ago, they threatened her and hauled her before government officials. But now, after she's walked with Christ for so long, no one tries to intimidate her anymore. She's a living testimony of the Spirit's power to sustain his people through difficulty and persecution.

Still, she's the only one left.

About twenty years ago, missionaries came to her little town, and a handful of people confessed Christ. Some were baptized, and the missionaries were filled with hope. Perhaps this was the beginning of a breakthrough, and the gospel would begin to spread! And then, for various reasons, the missionaries left, and the little group of believers began to fall apart. Abdul-Raheem had been baptized, but when he got into an ill-advised argument with some Muslims about his new faith, they dragged him to the mosque, beat him, and said they'd kill him if he didn't return to Islam. Bruised and terrified, he recited the Muslim creed and never spoke about Christ again. Mahmoud, too, returned to Islam. He came to Fatime's hut and returned his New Testament. Fatime knows all their stories. Two who remained faithful died in the past few years. But the majority? Fatime sighs, squints at me through her opaque eyes, and says, "They were afraid. Afraid of people."

But Fatime? She's been through it all. She's endured opposition and found God faithful. She's not afraid of anything anymore.

Suffering and Persecution in the Unreached World

This story may not surprise you. Sad things happen. People make unfortunate decisions, and not all seeds that spring up bear lasting fruit. But what if I suggested that the fear and persecution that caused Fatime's friends to return to Islam isn't unique? What if I suggested that it reflects a larger reality that people must face if they want to follow Christ in most of the world's unreached places?

Imagine flying over these places. You start in Morocco and wind your way over the North African deserts and the Arabian Peninsula, passing above the Persian Gulf, the Indian subcontinent, and China. Next, you swing south to cross over Thailand and then east to the tip of Indonesia. As the unreached peoples beneath you change from Muslim to Hindu to atheist to Buddhist to animist and back to Muslim again, one thing remains the same: In every place, the threat of persecution looms large over enormous groups of people who remain unreached by the gospel of Jesus Christ. It seems the hostile opposition to the gospel that unreached peoples live under may be as much a part of what blinds them to the truth as the formal teachings of Islam, Hinduism, Buddhism, or state-sponsored atheism. Similarly, it seems that suffering and persecution may be among the greatest threats to the growth and survival of churches in the least-reached areas. Indeed, areas that are both unreached by the gospel and exempt from persecution are the exceptions that prove the rule, especially when we realize that not only violence and martyrdom but also ostracism, humiliation, and rejection from families are potent and painful forms of persecution (e.g., Matt. 5:11–12; Heb. 10:33; 1 Pet. 2:23).[1]

Reports from believers in least-reached areas confirm what we've observed. Don Little shares that the three most common challenges Muslim-background believers report in their spiritual growth are all related to persecution.[2] That's certainly why so many who once professed faith return to Islam. Kevin Greeson writes, "Throughout the history of missionary outreach to Muslims, reconversion has been a persistent problem, with as many as 90 percent returning to Islam."[3] While Greeson cites no sources for his figure, most missionaries who have worked in the Muslim world would agree

1 While most of us can bear occasional name-calling, we may find being rejected or condemned by our loved ones or our wider society more painful than many types of physical persecution, and the New Testament pays extensive attention to the difficulty of bearing rejection.

2 Don Little, *Effective Discipling in Muslim Communities: Scripture, History and Seasoned Practices* (IVP Academic, 2015), chap. 9, Kindle.

3 Kevin Greeson, *The Camel: How Muslims Are Coming to Faith in Christ!* (WIGTake Resources, 2010), Appendix 1, Kindle.

with his claim. In India, Hindu nationalist *Ghar Wapsi* (literally, "returning home") programs using social and economic pressures as well as the threat of violent persecution have resulted in mass conversions back to Hinduism.[4]

Suffering is not only a problem for new believers in unreached areas but also a significant obstacle for missionaries. Most missionaries—especially those headed to poverty-stricken, disease-endemic areas—have much to consider before heading to the field. All Christians are called to love Christ more than wealth or family (Matt. 6:19–21; 10:37) and must be willing to leave "houses or brothers or sisters or father or mother or children or lands" (Matt. 19:29) for Jesus's sake. But missionaries often find themselves having to obey this command in the most literal sense. In some cases, their families may react with accusations and rejection. Then, once they arrive on the field, there are the slow trials of cultural disorientation, loneliness, and language learning.

When missionaries work in poverty-stricken environments, sickness usually awaits. Most of the missionaries Fatime knew left the field permanently when they encountered serious medical problems. Stationed two days' journey away from the nearest major hospital, they had little other choice. My wife and I minister in the same town where they worked, and we also encounter health challenges. As I write this, a teammate is recovering from her first bout of dengue fever. She was unable to get out of bed or open her eyes because of the pain. A few months ago, my wife and I woke up to find our one-year-old crying. He had a mysterious fever that spiked to 106 degrees Fahrenheit. There was no emergency number to call and no quick ambulance ride to an urgent care facility. We

4 Vijay Simha, "How to Be Un-Born Again," *Christianity Today,* November 10, 2008, https://www.christianitytoday.com.

were terrified, lost, and helpless, hanging in the hands of a God who would surely do good but had every right to decide that doing good meant asking us to bear the unbearable. I remember praying, "God, I have no words to express how much I need your mercy right now. Please bring this fever down. Please, please, please."

Missionaries may also face the acute sufferings of rejection, hostility, persecution, imprisonment, expulsion from their countries of service, and even martyrdom. This doesn't mean missionaries will necessarily suffer more than all other Christians or that their lives will primarily be defined by suffering. But it does mean they will regularly encounter serious obstacles that slow them down on their path to the unreached or even, God forbid, stop them altogether.

In the next chapter, we examine whether the Scriptures confirm that suffering and persecution pose a fundamental challenge to missionary efforts. For now, it's enough to note that a purely pragmatic look at the world—and at what missionaries and new believers in unreached contexts are telling us—*seems* to suggest that suffering and persecution are among the largest obstacles to Christian missionary endeavors.

What Is a Theology of Suffering, and Why Do We Need It?

Of course, most missionaries have accepted that a certain amount of suffering awaits them and those who come to Christ through their ministries. And if you were to watch them up close for several years, as I have, you would see that they certainly have a robust *respect* for suffering. They strive to suffer well, often at great personal cost. They speak of suffering with an almost reverent seriousness.

But it's not enough to approach suffering with respect. As much as we can, we also need to understand it. D. A. Carson notes that when tragedy strikes, if our beliefs "are largely out of step with the God who has disclosed himself in the Bible and supremely in Jesus, then the pain from personal tragedy may be multiplied many times over as we begin to question the very foundations of our faith."[5]

So we need a well-formed theology of suffering, which we can roughly define as an understanding of (1) God's broader purposes for suffering and (2) the roles that suffering plays for good and for evil in both the world and the Christian life. Suffering will catch us off guard if our deeper beliefs aren't formed by Scripture. We may collapse in surprise or sustain wounds and doubts that last longer than needed, or we may naively embrace unnecessary suffering that we're ill-equipped to handle. Our approach to suffering may be guided by romanticism or by a sense that we need to prove ourselves and the worthiness of our faith by suffering.

The need to teach clearly about suffering presses itself on us in questions that we hear echoing through the church and missionary life: *When is suffering necessary? When should it be avoided? What is its role in the Christian life? Why must we suffer when Christ has already suffered for us?* And perhaps most important, *How can we find strength to bear suffering when it comes?*

These questions are relevant to all Christians, and this book attempts to provide a brief theology of suffering that helps answer them. But because of the unique ways suffering may occur in mission-field settings, I want to pay special attention to its role in the lives of missionaries and the people they minister to. It's worth repeating: There's no scriptural warrant to assume missionaries will suffer more than other Christians. Nevertheless, the success of missionaries' ministries may depend, in large part, on the ma-

5 D. A. Carson, *How Long, O Lord? Reflections on Suffering and Evil*, 2nd ed. (Inter-Varsity Press, 2006), 11.

turity of their responses to the questions that arise when suffering comes. *When new believers refuse to confess their faith out of fear of persecution, how should we respond? When should we encourage new believers to flee from persecution? When should we encourage them to remain in their communities despite the threat of persecution? When missionaries are discouraged or depressed, should we encourage them to seek another vocation? Or should we encourage them to lean more heavily on Jesus?* Of course, these questions require wisdom. But a well-formed theology of suffering will not just leave appropriate room for gray areas, it will also draw black-and-white boundaries around them so we don't get lost in the grays.

A robust understanding of suffering is essential for missionaries. Countless books address how to share the gospel with Muslims, Hindus, and Buddhists, and they are vital for our missionary efforts. But we may need to focus just as much on learning how to share the gospel with people who know they will suffer if they accept it. Don Little reports that missionaries who have worked with Muslim-background believers recommended teaching a theology of persecution and suffering early in the discipleship process more frequently than they recommended teaching anything else.[6] Unfortunately, Little stops short of providing a systematic look at the Bible's major teachings about suffering and persecution. This isn't a criticism of Little's excellent book; no book can cover every topic. But it's generally true that books and training manuals for missionaries rarely explain how we might help new believers deal with the threat of persecution. Yes, missionaries are encouraged to tell new believers to count the cost, but that provides only an awareness that there is a price to pay for following Christ. It does little

6 Little, *Effective Discipling*, chap. 11.

to explain why that cost is necessary or to give the new believers hope to stand firm in the face of intimidation or brutal violence.

Many missionary responses seem to be colored with a sort of glib optimism: "The early church spread rapidly in highly persecuted contexts. Why should things be different today? Let's keep trusting Jesus and carry on." Certainly, trusting Jesus should always be at the center of our response to suffering. But trusting him in our sufferings includes believing that the things he taught us about suffering are vital to see us through and are worth studying in real depth. After all, we can't teach what we don't understand. So if we don't understand Jesus's teachings about suffering, we'll be unable to teach the nations to observe all that he commanded (Matt. 28:20). This will limit our ability to carry out the Great Commission.

Separateness and Suffering

Where do we begin if we want a scriptural understanding of suffering? It's true that Christians aren't the only people who suffer. As Job complains:

> Man is born to trouble
>   as the sparks fly upward. (Job 5:7)

While this world has its share of joys, Carson is right: "All we have to do is live long enough, and we will suffer."[7]

Yet there are special ways in which suffering affects God's people. God has always called his people to be separate from the world, forgoing many of its pleasures and the sense of acceptance and security it offers in order to seek an unseen inheritance from him. "Go," the

7 Carson, *How Long, O Lord?*, 16.

Lord told Abraham, "from your country and your kindred and your father's house to the land that I will show you" (Gen. 12:1). Moses left Egypt because he "considered the reproach of Christ greater wealth than the treasures of Egypt" (Heb. 11:26). God told Israel:

> Depart, depart, go out from there;
> touch no unclean thing;
> go out from the midst of her; purify yourselves,
> you who bear the vessels of the LORD. (Isa. 52:11)

The New Testament calls today's church to a similar separateness:

> Therefore go out from their midst,
> and be separate from them, says the Lord,
> and touch no unclean thing;
> then I will welcome you,
> and I will be a father to you,
> and you shall be sons and daughters to me,
> says the Lord Almighty. (2 Cor. 6:17–18)

> Do not love the world or the things in the world. If anyone loves the world, the love of the Father is not in him. (1 John 2:15)

When we separate ourselves from the world, the suffering we experience as a result is a uniquely Christian experience.

Of course, we aren't called "to go out of the world" or to stop associating with unbelievers (1 Cor. 5:10–11). Our task is more complex. We're called to remain here on earth but live as "strangers and exiles" who "desire a better country, that is, a heavenly one" (Heb. 11:13, 16).

The world does not appreciate having "strangers and exiles" in its midst. For example, when Fatime's wider community rejected her, it did so because it was shocked and angered by the ways she professed to live entirely beyond the control of its Islamic leaders and traditions. This should not surprise us. Jesus told us that a church that is separate from the world will be hated by the world. When and where the world can, it will persecute those it hates. As Jesus says:

> If you were of the world, the world would love you as its own; but because you are not of the world, but I chose you out of the world, therefore the world hates you. Remember the word that I said to you, "A servant is not greater than his master." If they persecuted me, they will also persecute you. (John 15:19–20)

Indeed, the "strangers and exiles" spoken of in Hebrews "suffered mocking and flogging, and even chains and imprisonment. They were stoned, they were sawn in two, they were killed with the sword. They went about in skins of sheep and goats, destitute, afflicted, mistreated" (Heb. 11:36–37). In many parts of the world, similar sufferings still await people who put their faith in Christ.

Today, the consequences of the church's separation from the world are becoming increasingly clear even in countries with historically Christian roots. Statistically, parts of post-Christian Europe could now be considered "unreached," and, not surprisingly, hostility toward Christian teaching in these areas has increased. In the United States, practicing Christians still constitute a substantial minority of the population. Nonetheless, hostility has steadily increased toward orthodox Christian doctrines and practices over the last few decades. It would be a serious overreaction to compare the difficulties American Christians endure with the problems Christians face in North Korea or in parts of India or Saudi Arabia. But it's equally an *underreaction* to assume that the hostility many non-Christians in the West feel toward the church is of little spiritual significance or that the West is too "civilized" and educated for persecution to become widespread and violent in future generations. It should not surprise us if we see persecution increasing as long as the post-Christian West continues to move away from Christianity and to more closely resemble a mission field.

Conclusion

In sum, suffering seems to be a normal part of walking with Christ, especially for those who follow him in areas with few or no believers. Missionaries in these areas need a deep and scripturally grounded theology of suffering. The following chapters provide just that. I look primarily to Scripture, but I also share stories from my own observations and experience. As I do, I'm deeply conscious that suffering takes different forms in different contexts and that my observations are limited. Nevertheless, the authors of the New Testament give us principles to describe the role suffering plays in the lives of believers. I share stories from my experience only to offer practical examples of how these principles play out in the lives and ministries of missionaries. Lastly, I draw on the insights of Christians who have gone before us. Our predecessors—who lived before both aspirin and psychotherapy and who, in many cases, endured harsh persecution—were often forced to understand suffering in ways few of us would imagine are necessary.

Here I'd like to briefly describe my approach to help readers engage with me along the way. First, when I discuss *missions* in this book, I use the term in a narrow sense to describe *the planting of churches that are mature enough to endure and multiply among people who previously had little or no access to the gospel.* People use the term *missions* in various circles to describe different types of ministries. Many of these other ministries are good and essential parts of the church's work, but it's beyond the scope of a single book to describe them all. I also don't assume that missionaries must be Westerners, and I rejoice to see a growing number of non-Western missionaries on the field. Because of the geographical and demographic distribution of least-reached peoples today, however, missions work among them, by definition, usually involves crossing cultural and linguistic boundaries and often involves crossing international borders.

Second, when we attempt to develop a deeper theology of suffering, most contemporary approaches begin with the problem of *theodicy*: "How could a good God allow suffering in his world?" This is a worthwhile question, but the New Testament writers seem mostly uninterested in answering it. They never ponder what greater good may have convinced an otherwise reluctant God to allow evil into his world. So while questions of theodicy are worthwhile to address, they shouldn't be our primary focus as we develop a scriptural theology of suffering. In fact, questions that begin with "How could a good God . . ." are profoundly limited because they're bent toward accusation.[8] They attempt to evaluate God's larger character with a laser-like focus on an aspect of his dealing with the world which troubles us and that Scripture warns is beyond our ability

8 These questions are inherently accusatory in nature and skew the discussion that follows. If I were to initiate a discussion with my wife by asking, "How could a good wife and mother behave in this way?" anyone who overheard the question would recognize the accusation behind it and would see her resulting defensiveness as a natural response. Additionally, these questions are based on the implicit and undefended assumption that humans would be able to understand God's purposes for allowing suffering in the world—an assumption the Scriptures strongly contest, especially in the book of Job.

to fully understand (see Job 38–42). This leaves us, at best, carving out room for the possibility that God *could* still be good despite the evil in the world. Little room is left to argue proactively for his abundant goodness.

The writers of the New Testament have a less defensive and more pragmatic focus. Rather than losing themselves in abstract essays that speculate about whether the world would have been better—and God would have been more righteous—if suffering had never occurred, they tell us a story about what God is doing to redeem our suffering. In this story, suffering and evil emerge as temporary and insubstantial realities in comparison with the eternal, glorious redemption God will bring about (e.g., Rom. 8:18; 2 Cor. 4:17–18). Ultimately, the Scriptures tell us that God's redemption will lead us through suffering and evil to a joy that swallows them up entirely. The Scriptures compare this to the way that the suffering of childbirth is swallowed up by the joy of a baby being born (e.g., John 16:21–22; Rom. 8:18–22). We see this redemption of suffering most clearly in the resurrection of Jesus Christ. Christ's resurrection not only reverses his death, it swallows up death entirely for all God's children, forever.

The New Testament writers repeatedly hold up Christ's suffering and reward as a pattern to encourage us. They rarely speak of suffering without speaking about joy and reward, and they seem to believe there is an inextricable link between the two (cf. Rom. 5:3; Col. 1:24; Heb. 10:34; 1 Pet. 4:12–13).

In contrast, when today's missionary literature speaks of suffering, it tends to emphasize counting the cost. We err on the side of encouraging people to tough it out and get serious. And certainly, counting the cost is necessary. But cost is only one side of any good decision, and it's the less important side at that! Should we not focus more fully, as the Scriptures do, on the joy and reward that Jesus promises?

It's precisely here that our attempt to build a theology of suffering will take a surprising turn. Joy and suffering seem to go hand in hand. Importantly, suffering is not the point: joy is. Suffering is only the road; joy is the destination. God calls us to be separate from the world but only so that we can inherit something better. A theology of suffering, then, is only one facet of a larger theology of joy, and it may be impossible to really come through suffering well without keeping this in mind.

Here's a brief road map of where we are going. First, chapter 2 examines suffering and explores its origins in our world. Then, in chapters 3–4, we consider the strange, surprising connection the Scriptures draw between suffering and joy. Finally, we spend chapters 5–7 exploring how missionaries and churches must react to suffering in order to faithfully pursue Christ's Great Commission in persecuted contexts.

From beginning to end, I'll try to keep our focus aligned with the Scriptures. I don't believe our task is limited to developing a theology of suffering. Instead, our task is to develop a theology of godly joy and, as part of that, to understand why suffering is necessary to lead us there. If this is true of the Christian life, then it's certainly true of the church's missionary task.

2

Suffering, Slavery, and the Rule of Satan

The wicked and deceitful spirit, the serpent, will not cease putting to death and persecuting those who confess Christ until he come again.

JUSTIN MARTYR
Dialogue with Trypho

FOR MONTHS, refugees were trickling into the little border town where my wife and I work. That all changed unexpectedly one Wednesday afternoon when the refugees' governor used the word "genocide" to describe what was happening to his people. Within a few hours, he was kidnapped and murdered by the militias whose actions he denounced. Refugees began flooding across the border—tens of thousands and then hundreds of thousands. I hope you never see anything like it. They came naked, wounded, and bleeding. Our little town swelled into a city. In the end, hundreds of thousands of refugees were registered in our town alone. They built a tent city outside our town, using shelters made of sticks, pieces of cloth, torn tarps—whatever they could find.

And then they began to tell their stories.

The refugees were attacked by militias as they fled. The militias ignored international law and killed all the men they could find. And it wasn't just men that they killed. They slaughtered women, the elderly, and children too. Those they did not kill were assaulted, beaten, robbed, stripped, and tortured. In one particularly heart-rending case, a woman fled carrying her infant son on her back, and the militants who found her clubbed her son to death and let her go. It was a cruel sort of game to them: "That'll teach you not to come back."

I remember how vividly those days reminded me that the suffering in the world is not random. It is not simply the result of bad luck or bad policy. The abuses we saw were intentional. They were evil, malicious, and meticulous. These horrific events were planned. Even the nonreligious described the crimes we observed as "demonic."

In this chapter, I want to take their conclusion a step further. I argue that demonic malice was instrumental in bringing all kinds of suffering into our world. This is true not only of suffering that occurs directly through obvious human sinfulness, like the ethnic cleansing and refugee crisis that my wife and I observed, but also of the suffering that occurs through earthquakes, divorce, bereavement, car accidents, or even arthritis. None of these would exist apart from the fall, and Satan's deception was instrumental in enticing Eve (and then Adam) to sin (1 Tim. 2:13–14), which brought futility and bondage to the world (Rom. 8:20–21).

In arguing this, I recognize that all events ultimately come about through God's ordination and planning, even when they involve people or demons rebelling against God.[1] However, there can be multiple layers of causation—not only divine but also human and even demonic—and as we will see, we need to be aware of them all.

This should not lead to a superstitious "devil behind every bush" theology that causes us to see every head cold and stubbed toe as the result of a deeper diabolical plan. The devil doesn't have to directly and consciously cause each specific sickness or misfortune that befalls us for all human sickness and misfortune to find its origin in his work and in the disorder and fallenness he helped to introduce into creation. Scripturally, as we will see, suffering and death are Satan's design, and he has dark purposes that he intends them to accomplish.[2] Specifically, we saw in the previous chapter that God calls his people to be separate from the world. Satan, on the other hand, uses suffering to keep God's people in bondage.

1 For example, in Acts 2:23, Peter states that the crucifixion of Jesus occurred "according to the definite plan and foreknowledge of God."

2 Throughout this chapter I do not differentiate between the work of Satan and the work of demons more generally. Scripture alternates between describing suffering and death as caused by Satan (e.g., Luke 13:16; Heb. 2:14–15; Rev. 2:10) and describing them as caused by the powers or demons in general (e.g., Matt. 12:22; 1 Cor. 2:8; Eph. 1:20–21). As an evangelical writing primarily for an evangelical audience, I speak about Satan and the demons as personal beings, at least to the extent of having their own thoughts and purposes that drive their actions. I'm aware here that many readers, even those who are very familiar with the Bible, may have grotesque ideas or comical caricatures of devils in their minds. These ideas will distract them by rendering the scriptural narrative so fantastical and fairy-tale-like that they will either reject it or, having embraced it, will find it largely irrelevant to the real-life world we inhabit. So I'm asking readers to put aside any distracting, cartoonish images of the devil and listen to the story the Scriptures tell about suffering in our world. To the extent that we need to understand Satan or other demonic beings, we can do so only by attending at least partly to their actions in this story. We won't easily understand what a great evil human suffering is without understanding that the scriptural story presents suffering as entering our world not by chance but through the intentional actions of malevolent forces.

Suffering in the Scriptural Narrative

Scripture begins with God creating a good world and appointing humans to establish his generous rule over creation (Gen. 1:27–28). When humans failed to do so by listening to the serpent and falling into sin (Gen. 3:1–7), they ceded dominion over creation to Satan (Matt. 4:8–9; 1 Cor. 5:5). Thus, he is described as both "the ruler of this world" (John 12:31; 14:30) and "the god of this world" (2 Cor. 4:4). Today, "the whole world lies in the power of the evil one" (1 John 5:19), and he's filled it with suffering and death. It's only after he gained a foothold in the garden that humanity was cursed with relational strife, painful toil, agony in childbirth, and death (Gen. 3:16–19). And it's no coincidence that immediately after the devil will be judged (Rev. 20:10), death itself will be done away with (Rev. 20:14), and a new world will be ushered in with no "mourning, nor crying, nor pain" (Rev. 21:4).

Moreover, death is the ultimate and archetypal human suffering, and Hebrews describes the devil as having "the power of death" (Heb. 2:14). Paul, too, links death with the authorities and powers—which is Paul's terminology for demonic powers. That's why it's through the victory of Jesus and his saints over death (Col. 2:12–13) that God "disarmed the rulers and authorities and put them to open shame, by triumphing over them in him" (Col. 2:15).[3] Elsewhere, Paul writes, "Then comes the end, when he delivers the kingdom to God the Father after destroying every rule and every authority and power. For he must reign until he has put all his

3 See Eph. 2:1–2; 6:12. Similarly, it is only after mentioning how "we are being killed all the day long" that Paul notes that "neither death . . . nor angels nor rulers . . . nor powers" can separate us from Christ's love (Rom. 8:36–38). Paul connects the danger of death that his readers face with the actions of the rulers and powers.

enemies under his feet. The last enemy to be destroyed is death" (1 Cor. 15:24–26).

Within this larger narrative, the Scriptures are filled with specific stories in which Satan causes suffering. Importantly, Satan is described as causing not only the suffering that comes as a direct result of human wickedness but also the seemingly "random" suffering that comes from natural disasters and disease. It is Satan who uses a great storm to kill Job's children and strikes him "with loathsome sores from the sole of his foot to the crown of his head" (Job 2:7). Similarly, in the New Testament, Matthew and Luke depict muteness, blindness, and seizures as caused by demons (Matt. 9:32–34; 12:22–24; 17:15; Luke 4:35; 11:14–15). Jesus himself describes a woman disabled for eighteen years as bound by Satan in her sickness (Luke 13:16). Clearly, as the Scriptures show, physical illness is sometimes a result of satanic or demonic activity.

Today, many Christians imagine that certain sicknesses have physical causes and should be treated medically while other illnesses are caused by demons and can be cured through exorcism. I don't think this is what the Gospel writers mean, since they almost always speak of healings and the casting out of demons in the same breath (e.g., Matt. 4:24; 10:8; Mark 1:32, 34; Luke 9:1). Those who have power to do one have power to do the other. The Gospel writers see sickness more broadly as tied to the work of demons. Of course, sickness still has physical causes, but under the broader umbrella of God's sovereignty, it is the devil's work that sets them in motion to bring about human suffering, even if this often occurs only indirectly as a result of the fall. That said, the devil can act to cause suffering directly—in Job's case, Satan works through physical causes to take Job's livestock, kill his children, and produce intense physical pain.

Here, I'd like to offer two clarifications. First, I recognize that some readers might be confused when I say that the Scriptures point to Satan as the initiator of human suffering. Don't the Scriptures also describe God as sovereign over all suffering and death? After all, God says:

> See now that I, even I, am he,
> and there is no god beside me;
> I kill and I make alive;
> I wound and I heal. (Deut. 32:39)

And Satan is able to torment Job only when God gives him permission to do so (Job 1:1–12; 2:4–6).

We can recognize several layers of causation as we discuss this topic. It's true that suffering and death were *ordained* by God, but it was still through Satan's work that they entered human history. After all, while God curses humans with suffering and death in the garden, he does so only after they rebel and listen to the serpent (Gen. 3:14–19). Thus, while we see both God and Satan at work in people's suffering in the Scriptures, God and Satan stand behind that suffering asymmetrically. For Satan, suffering and death are ends in themselves; for God, they are corrective measures that he uses to judge the evil that has occurred in this suffering world and to redeem his people from it. He is leading his people through suffering to a new world where "death shall be no more, neither shall there be mourning, nor crying, nor pain anymore" (Rev. 21:4).

But suffering is only a part of our redemption because of Satan's rule in our world. For example, Paul writes, "So to keep me from becoming conceited because of the surpassing greatness of the revelations, a thorn was given me in the flesh, a messenger of Satan to harass me, to keep me from becoming conceited" (2 Cor. 12:7). Clearly, God bestowed a physical ailment on Paul, and he did so for Paul's sake. But again, because Paul's thorn caused destruction and suffering in his body, it was not only a gift from God but also a "messenger of Satan." People wouldn't need thorns in their flesh to keep them humble if the world hadn't been marred by the work of Satan.

Second, when I say that all suffering and death are largely the result of Satan's work, I am not taking issue with the traditional evangelical position that human suffering finds its origin in human sinfulness. Here again, it's important to remember that multiple layers of causation can operate simultaneously. D. A. Carson rightly observes that "the first human rebellion (Gen. 3) marks the onset of suffering, pain, toil, and death. . . . Evil is the primal cause of suffering, rebellion is the root of pain, sin is the source of death."[4]

I agree entirely that human suffering and death entered the world through human sinfulness. I'm simply asking readers to remember, in addition, that humans fell into sin only after being tempted by Satan in the garden. Thus, both human sinfulness *and* the devil's work are instrumental in causing human suffering. It's important that we acknowledge both realities. If we insist that human suffering is *merely* a result of human sinfulness—introduced into the world by God either to correct and punish human sin or to establish a natural consequence for sin—then we'll miss the malicious demonic purposes that operate alongside God's own good purposes in our suffering. Maintaining an awareness of these darker

4 D. A. Carson, *How Long, O Lord? Reflections on Suffering and Evil*, 2nd ed. (Inter-Varsity Press, 2006), 39. Similarly, Tim Keller writes, "It is fair to say that suffering and death in general is a natural consequence and just judgment of God on our sin." Timothy Keller, *Walking with God Through Pain and Suffering* (Hodder & Stoughton, 2015), 411.

purposes will help us both resist them and understand how great an evil human suffering is.

Persecution as Satan's Instrument

As we saw earlier, Satan is able to pour out suffering and death on the earth only because humans ceded their dominion and allowed him to take control. Today, missionaries are sent out as ambassadors to take back the earth by Jesus's authority. Note what Jesus says:

> I saw Satan fall like lighting from heaven. Behold, I have given you authority to tread on serpents and scorpions, and over all the power of the enemy. (Luke 10:18–19)

> All authority in heaven and on earth has been given to me. Go therefore and make disciples of all nations. (Matt. 28:18–19)

And yet a great deal of humanity is still under Satan's control, so he works together with people and uses persecution to oppose the spread of Jesus's kingdom.

My friend Ismael was fourteen years old when he decided to follow Christ. His family didn't like his decision, so they tied him up and discussed whether to kill him. In those terrible moments, Ismael's family wasn't acting only on their own malice. Instead, the Scriptures indicate that there was a darker hatred behind their actions that they may not have even fully grasped. The New Testament repeatedly lays the cause of persecution at Satan's feet. Let's look at a number of biblical examples.

Just before Jesus's death, he says, "The ruler of this world is coming" (John 14:30). Of course, the devil didn't physically show up and arrest Jesus. But he was behind the soldiers who did. In fact, Jesus's arrest was set in motion only when "the devil . . . put it into the heart of Judas Iscariot, Simon's son, to betray him" (John 13:2). That's why Jesus himself can tell his enemies, "You seek to kill me. . . . You are doing the works your father did. . . . You are of your father the devil, and your will is to do your father's desires" (John 8:40–44).

In 1 Peter 5:8–9, when Peter addresses the "suffering [that is] being experienced" by first-century churches, he doesn't say, "Rome prowls around like a roaring lion, seeking someone to devour." No, he says, "Your adversary the devil prowls around like a roaring lion, seeking someone to devour." Why? Because he knows the devil is behind Rome's persecution of the churches.

When Paul and his companions are driven out of Thessalonica, he doesn't say that persecution hindered him from coming back to see the Thessalonians. No, he says, "Satan hindered us" (1 Thess. 2:18). Why? because he knows Satan is behind the persecution.

In 1 John 3:12, we read that Cain "was of the evil one and murdered his brother . . . [b]ecause his own deeds were evil and his brother's righteous." Why does he say this? Because he knows it was the devil's grip on Cain that motivated him to murder Abel.

In Revelation, when Jesus speaks to the church of Smyrna, he doesn't tell them that Rome will throw some of them into prison to be tested. No, he says, "Behold, the devil is about to throw some of you into prison, that you may be tested, and for ten days you will have tribulation" (Rev. 2:10). He tells the church of Pergamum that Antipas "was killed among you, where Satan dwells" (Rev. 2:13). So Antipas's death was the result of Satan's work through the people who killed him.

Later on in Revelation, we're told that "the dragon . . . went off to make war on . . . those who keep the commandments of God and hold to the testimony of Jesus" (Rev. 12:17). The dragon gives his power to the beast (Rev. 13:2) and enables him to "make war on the saints and to conquer them. And authority was given it over every tribe and people and language and nation, and all who dwell on earth will worship it, everyone whose name has not been written from the foundation of the world in the book of life of the Lamb who was slain" (Rev. 13:7–8). We can't afford to miss what's happening in this passage. In a terrible sort of reverse Great Commission, the beast uses persecution to seize the authority that rightfully belongs to Jesus over "every tribe and language and people and nation" (Rev. 5:9; cf. 7:9). Persecution can deliver entire nations over to Satan.

Viewed together, the examples above show that the New Testament authors repeatedly attribute persecution to Satan's work. For those who worry that what I have said about persecution may lead to a superstitious overemphasis on the role of Satan and demonic powers, I would respond again that the New Testament never insists that Satan directly and consciously incites each act of persecution that takes place or each harsh word spoken against a follower of Christ. Rather, Satan is "the deceiver of the whole world" (Rev. 12:9). The New Testament leaves room for cases in which Satan is directly inciting persecution and other cases in which people he has deceived persecute others without his direct incitement.

Satan's Purposes for Suffering and Persecution

But how is Satan able to use persecution so effectively? How is he able to deceive entire nations with the simple threat of suffering and violence?

Earlier, I said it's important for us to understand Satan's malicious purposes in our suffering so that we might be able to resist them. Specifically, the Scriptures suggest that Satan uses suffering and persecution to undermine people's faith in God. Before Satan causes Job to suffer, he says, "Does Job fear God for no reason? . . . You have blessed the work of his hands, and his possessions have increased in the land. But stretch out your hand and touch all that he has, and he will curse you to your face" (Job 1:9–11; see also 2:4–5). Why does Satan think Job will curse God if he suffers? It is because he knows that if Job's suffering is intense enough, Job will feel that God has forsaken him. Satan is coming for Job's faith. The following chapters in the book of Job record Job's struggle with this temptation in painful detail, as he wonders how God could be good and allow suffering to befall the righteous.

Suffering always carries with it a temptation to unbelief, which is why Satan tempts Jesus to doubt God's fatherly love when he's near starvation (Matt. 4:3).

If this is true of suffering more generally, then it's especially true of the suffering caused by persecution. We see an example of how this works when Hebrews tells us Jesus died so that "through death he might destroy the one who has the power of death, that is, the devil, and deliver all those who through fear of death were subject to lifelong slavery" (Heb. 2:14–15).

In order to understand this passage, we need to remember that the author of Hebrews is writing to encourage early believers who are facing persecution, including imprisonment and the confiscation of their property (Heb. 10:32–34; 13:3). The author's repeated concern for them is that they "hold fast" their confession and hope (see Heb. 3:6; 4:14; 6:18; 10:23). Although they haven't yet faced martyrdom, some may face it soon (Heb. 12:4). So he encourages the believers to fix their eyes on Jesus, the one who endured death and was richly rewarded (Heb. 12:1–2). In context, then, when Hebrews 2:15 says that Satan enslaves people "through fear of death," the author is speaking about the terror of death by persecution that can enslave people and leave them unable to follow Christ. This is even clearer in the following chapter when the author of Hebrews warns his readers against falling into the sins of their forefathers:

> Do not harden your hearts as in the rebellion,
> on the day of testing in the wilderness. (Heb. 3:8)

The "day of testing in the wilderness" is a reference to the rebellion at Massah and Meribah, where the Israelites said, "Why did you bring us up out of Egypt, to kill us and our children and our livestock with thirst?" (Ex. 17:3).[5]

Do you see the comparison the author of Hebrews is drawing? The fear of death caused the Israelites to lose faith in God's good intentions toward them and made them want to return to slavery in Egypt. The author of Hebrews doesn't want his readers to make the same mistake. He doesn't want their fear of death to make them return to the slavery of the devil. He concludes this section by warning his readers to "take care, brothers, lest there be in any of you an evil, unbelieving heart" (Heb. 3:12). Put simply, Satan uses persecution to sow unbelief in people's hearts.

Perhaps the clearest example of this is found in Satan's temptation of Peter. Just before Peter denies Christ, Jesus says, "Simon, Simon, behold, Satan demanded to have you, that he might sift

5 In Heb. 3:7–12, the author warns his readers not to return to slavery due to the fear of death. Instead of quoting Ex. 17:7, where the narrative occurs, he quotes Ps. 95:7–11. Psalm 95 discusses the incident at Massah and Meribah in the context of singing praises to God and offering true repentance to him.

you like wheat, but I have prayed for you that your faith may not fail" (Luke 22:31–32). If we keep reading, we realize that it is *through the fear of death* that Satan tries to "have" Peter. As Jesus is about to be crucified, the devil terrifies Peter so that he no longer sees how God could deliver him from death, and Peter forgets that God will take care of him even if he dies with Jesus. Once upon a time, Peter earnestly hoped to stand with Jesus (John 13:37), but when the time comes, he's no longer able—or willing—to do so. He denies Christ.

It's worth mentioning that the devil wants more than Peter's denial: He's coming for Peter's faith. That's why Jesus prays that Peter's faith won't fail. Satan is coming to "sift" Peter, and he hopes that when persecution shakes out the chaff from Peter's faith, no real wheat will be left. Thankfully, Peter's faith doesn't fail, but we can see why Jesus says that this was what the devil was trying to accomplish. At the most obvious level, Christ's crucifixion was cruel Roman street theater intended to warn people not to tangle with Rome. But it was more. At a deeper and darker level, it was also a kind of demonic street theater designed to tell Peter and others who would follow Jesus, "Don't trust the God that Jesus worshiped. He can't rescue you from us."

Years ago, I remember listening as my friends Ayman and Juma were talking. "I'd love to read the New Testament sometime to see what it says," Ayman commented to Juma. Juma responded, "If you did, people would think you were a Christian. And they would take your wife and kids away." When I asked what this meant, they explained to me that because Ayman had married his wife as a Muslim man, leaving Islam would mean that his marriage would likely be annulled by the community. What a powerful deception! Satan need not deceive Ayman into thinking Jesus's claims are incorrect if he can deceive him into thinking that it's not worth jeopardizing his family by learning about Jesus in the first place.

During the refugee crisis I described at the beginning of this chapter, a handful of refugees expressed interest in Christ. I remember inviting a young man named Abdul-Aziz to study the Bible with me. He looked at the ground and said, "I really want to leave Islam. But Matt, I'm scared. People might do bad things to me." He paused and looked up at me, "They might even kill me." His fears weren't entirely unfounded. Everyone I've seen from our area who has turned away from Islam and toward Christ has suffered for it. What a terrible trap. Satan has not only turned this world into a violent place where ethnic cleansing and refugee crises happen; he has also used the threat of violence to stop people from finding Christ, the one who might give them the strength to resist such evils.

We need to understand, then, that the spiritual warfare we endure is not *merely* spiritual. It certainly has spiritual causes, but it largely plays out in very tangible ways. Satan uses persecution to wage war against God's people. By explaining this, I hope to remove some of the "spookiness" that has attached itself to our understanding of spiritual warfare. I don't mean that our enemy is less wicked than we imagined. I simply intend to highlight the fact that he wages war against us largely through earthly, human means. After all, it is the earth that he seeks to rule and humans that he seeks to destroy.[6]

6 Ephesians 6:12 could seem to suggest otherwise: "For we do not wrestle against flesh and blood, but against the rulers, against the authorities, against the cosmic powers over this present darkness, against the spiritual forces of evil in the heavenly places." Certainly, Paul is stating that our struggles are caused by unseen spiritual powers. But nothing in the passage indicates that these spiritual struggles don't often play out in visible ways in the physical world. Indeed, Paul's hope in this passage is that the Ephesians "may be able to withstand in the evil day [*en tē hēmera tē ponēra*]" (Eph. 6:13). The phrase "evil day" is quoted

This is why we never see New Testament believers battling the devil by "binding" demonic powers that haunt certain nations, territories, or buildings. We never see them engaging in spiritual warfare by releasing people from "generational curses." We do, however, see them frequently referring to spiritual struggles as they face persecution. Jesus says to Pilate, "My kingdom is not of this world. If my kingdom were of this world, my servants would have been fighting, that I might not be delivered over to the Jews. But my kingdom is not from the world" (John 18:36). Satan's kingdom, however, is very much of this world: He's the "ruler of this world" (John 14:30), and his servants are fighting because he's largely limited to the means of this world to rule the world. His attempts at power are governed by the "wisdom of this age" since he is one of "the rulers of this age" (1 Cor. 2:6–8). Like any worldly despot, he turns quickly to violence when his power is challenged or his deception is uncovered. He does so by inciting worldly tyrants to violence. The systems of this world and their dog-eat-dog violence spread pain across the earth through the wickedness of powerful men. They're rooted directly in Satan's own violent nature; the children of the devil do their "father's desires," for "he was a murderer from the beginning" (John 8:44).

Suffering and Persecution as Normative Experiences in the Christian Life

Suffering and persecution are widespread and normal in the Christian life. Peter warns us, "Do not be surprised at the fiery trial when it

---

from the Septuagint (the Greek version of the Old Testament), where it is always used to describe suffering at the hand of our enemies: "In the day of trouble [*hēmera ponēra*] the LORD delivers him. . . . [Y]ou do not give him up to the will of his enemies" (Ps. 41:1–2; cf. 49:5; Jer. 17:17–18).

comes upon you to test you" (1 Pet. 4:12). Paul asserts that "through many tribulations we must enter the kingdom of God" (Acts 14:22). These verses don't mean that persecution and suffering happen with equal intensity in every Christian's life or at all points in history, but all Christians must be prepared to encounter them.

Of course, persecution isn't the only tool Satan uses to enslave the nations. But we can expect that where his rule is more firmly entrenched, he will stir up persecution more easily. Luke writes, "And the Lord said to Paul one night in a vision, 'Do not be afraid, but go on speaking and do not be silent, for I am with you, and no one will attack you to harm you, for I have many in this city who are my people' " (Acts 18:9–10). As the ruler of this world, Satan is partially dependent on the means of this world to incite persecution, working through public opinion, politics, force, wealth, and power. Therefore, where the Lord has many people, persecution may often be milder or lie dormant for periods of time. But in unreached settings, where the Lord has few people—or none—persecution might arise with surprising savagery.

Indeed, this is largely what we see in our world. In most unreached places, persecution is the norm. And where it appears to be mild, it can rapidly become more severe if people start turning to Christ. It is no coincidence, for example, that Nepal enacted antiproselytization laws after the church experienced massive growth during years of relatively open-minded government policies.[7]

Moreover, Satan can work through the fear of death to enslave people even if persecution stops short of martyrdom. The threat of lethal force is obvious when people are imprisoned, beaten, or

7 Office of International Religious Freedom, *2021 Report on International Religious Freedom: Nepal* (U.S. Department of State, 2021), https://www.state.gov/.

robbed for their faith. That's why the author of Hebrews goes to such lengths to encourage his readers not to fear death even though none of them have yet been killed (Heb. 12:4).

But if Satan can convince people not to believe in the resurrection—if he can convince them that death is final and is ultimately a fearful thing—then they will lack motivation to bear other sufferings too, even those that stop short of what the early readers of Hebrews endured. Why suffer humiliation and social rejection now if we won't receive a payoff in the next life? Those who don't think they can gain a better world for having been rejected in this one will have little motivation to live as "strangers and exiles on the earth" (Heb. 11:13). Similarly, people who don't expect to receive glory and an inclusion in the next life will have little motivation to "go to [Jesus] outside the camp and bear the reproach he endured" (Heb. 13:13). That's why Paul makes comments like these:

> If in Christ we have hope in this life only, we are of all people most to be pitied. (1 Cor. 15:19)

> If the dead are not raised at all, . . . [w]hy are we in danger every hour? . . . What do I gain if, humanly speaking, I fought with beasts at Ephesus? If the dead are not raised, "Let us eat and drink, for tomorrow we die." (1 Cor. 15:29–32)

So when I speak of the fear of death as the driving force through which persecution binds people in darkness, I'm not only addressing missionaries who live where martyrdom is a real possibility; I'm also addressing missionaries in all contexts where believers suffer for their faith.

Taking Suffering and Persecution Seriously

One of the distinctives of Christian teaching is that it takes suffering seriously and validates what we know from experience to be true. It confirms that suffering is entirely evil in itself and that God is against human suffering and will do away with it altogether in his new creation.[8] In contrast, Buddhist teachings portray suffering as a consequence of karma that balances out wrongdoing. Ultimately, a Buddhist is supposed to believe that suffering is an illusion brought on by unenlightened humanity's penchant for desire. Islam sees death and suffering not as results of sin but as tests instituted by God that all must endure, even—in many strands of Islam—the sinless angels.[9] Hinduism views both the instigators and victims of suffering as drops in the great sea that is god. Materialism sees suffering as an unfortunate but morally neutral product of random chemical and biological processes that play out in a survival-of-the-fittest world.

Only Christianity sees suffering as the work of a wicked power that has seized control of the earth and desires to devour all who live in it. And only Christianity acknowledges that it's entirely beyond our strength to weather serious suffering on our own. Its message to sufferers is not "Deal with it," "Man up," or "Rise to the challenge." We are like Peter on the night of Jesus's arrest: however

8 When I describe all suffering as evil, I do not mean that all suffering is sinful or malicious. Some causes of suffering—a typhoon, an earthquake, or even a stomachache—are impersonal events that are incapable of sin or malice. Rather, they are "evil" in the sense of "causing harm" or being "marked by misfortune." *Merriam-Webster Dictionary*, "evil," accessed January 28, 2025, https://www.merriam-webster.com. See the use of the term in Job 2:10. Additionally, suffering is "evil" because God himself intends to put an end to it for the redeemed and expects righteous people to do what they can to stand against it.

9 According to many branches of Islamic teaching, even angels (who have no sin) must eventually die before being resurrected, judged, and rewarded.

willing our spirits may be to face persecution, our flesh is often weak (Matt. 26:41). And David writes:

> If it had not been the Lord who was on our side
> when people rose up against us,
> then they would have swallowed us up alive,
> when their anger was kindled against us;
> then the flood would have swept us away,
> the torrent would have gone over us. (Ps. 124:2–4)

We are unable to endure real suffering without God's help.

There is a practical takeaway to all this. Sometimes love or obedience may call us to expose ourselves to suffering, and we explore when and why in the following chapters. But we should never seek out suffering for its own sake, and we should do what we can to alleviate the suffering of our brothers and sisters throughout the world. Suffering should never be idealized or romanticized. It's a great evil in the world. Certainly, it may be a necessary evil at times, but since God alone knows when suffering will serve his larger purposes, we should work against it and pray for it to end. When God sees fit to answer these prayers, we trust that he will still be at work to redeem the world in gentler ways.

Conclusion

In chapter 1, we observed that suffering and persecution seem to pose an enormous obstacle to the church's missionary efforts. In this chapter, we have confirmed that this is entirely consistent with Scripture. We've also begun to uncover a story that will provide us with foundations for a theology of suffering in missionary contexts:

- God created a good earth and gave humans dominion over it, but humans rebelled and ceded their dominion over the world to the devil.
- The devil's work has filled the world with suffering and death, and all suffering is an evil in our world.[10]
- Scripture repeatedly describes persecution as being instigated by the devil.
- For the devil, suffering is an end in itself. In contrast, God works in his people's sufferings, but his purpose in doing so is to bring the redeemed to a new heaven and a new earth that are free from suffering and evil (Rev. 21:1–4).
- The devil uses suffering—and especially the suffering that results from persecution—to tempt us to doubt God's goodness.
- The fear of persecution and death binds the earth's least reached peoples in unbelief.
- Because suffering is evil, we should seek to avoid it whenever we can.

Suffering and persecution ruin countless lives and are great stains on God's good creation. One day, God plans to rid creation of them forever, but for now, he is at work in his people's suffering. In the next two chapters, we examine the surprising ways in which God works to redeem creation for himself through the pain and destruction Satan has poured out on the earth. Indeed, this is the more significant side of the story, and until we understand it, we won't be able to understand the role suffering plays in the Christian life or in the expansion of God's kingdom.

10 See note 8 for my use of the term *evil.*

3

The New Exodus

Long journeys are attended with toil and fatigue. . . .
The land we have to travel through, is a wilderness; there are
many mountains, rocks and rough places we must go over.

JONATHAN EDWARDS
"The Christian Pilgrim, Or, The True Christian's
Life a Journey Toward Heaven"

MY TEAMMATE GREG was drinking tea with Sadiq, a local believer, when an angry neighbor surprised them by trying to crush Sadiq's head with a brick.

Sadiq had become a believer over a decade ago. When a powerful tribal leader heard about his conversion, he sentenced Sadiq to death. Thankfully, God spared his life, but Sadiq was rejected and impoverished, enduring years of mocking and insults. Initially, he wanted to respond angrily, but he eventually grew into an effective evangelist. Through his evangelism his neighbor's son responded to the gospel with interest—and that's why his neighbor tried to crush his head with a brick.

But Sadiq had not only grown as an evangelist, he also had grown into a gentler man. Years ago, Sadiq would have fought with his neighbor. But on this occasion, Greg restrained Sadiq's raging neighbor while Sadiq ran inside his house, weeping bitterly. He wept because it was humiliating, especially in his culture, for a man to run away from a fight. He wept because he was surrendering his anger to Jesus. He wept because he was exhausted and discouraged by the continuing toll of persecution. How long would it be until people let him live in peace?

When God calls us to separate ourselves from the world, he also calls us out of slavery and into freedom. But as we saw in the previous chapter, Satan uses suffering to discourage us from persevering on God's path to freedom. Sadiq's neighbor wanted to injure and terrify him, and Satan inspires such violence for the same purpose.

I want to be as clear as I can: We should never seek suffering, but we may have to bear suffering as we seek to be free. And for missionaries or for evangelists like Sadiq, we may also have to bear suffering as we call others to join us in our journey to freedom.

We follow Jesus's footsteps on this journey because Jesus suffered first to set us free. Hebrews tells us that Jesus died so that "through death he might destroy the one who has the power of death, that is, the devil, and deliver all those who through fear of death were subject to lifelong slavery" (Heb. 2:14–15). Many missionaries today emphasize "power encounters," which have been defined as "visible, practical demonstration[s] that Jesus Christ is more powerful than the spirits, powers, or false gods worshiped or feared by the members of a given people group."[1] It's true that "power

1 C. Peter Wagner, *Confronting the Powers* (Regal Books, 1996), 102.

encounters" occur at points in Jesus's ministry, but Jesus's greatest victory was won through a "weakness encounter."

How can a cross overpower the mighty? Satan and the powers[2] were completely unprepared for what happened. Although they are rulers of this world, they only have the wisdom of this age. Paul writes:

> But we preach Christ crucified, a stumbling block to Jews and folly to Gentiles, but to those who are called, both Jews and Greeks, Christ the power of God and the wisdom of God. . . . None of the rulers of this age understood this, for if they had, they would not have crucified the Lord of glory. (1 Cor. 1:23–24; 2:8)[3]

Paul isn't saying that God tricked Satan into having Jesus crucified in some sort of divine sting operation. Rather, he's saying that Jesus ushered in a new type of kingdom by wielding an entirely different kind of power that the world and its dark spiritual powers are unable to understand or overcome.

The contrast between Christ's kingdom and Satan's kingdom and their two types of power reaches its climax as Jesus stands before Pontius Pilate. When Pilate asks if Jesus is setting himself up as king, Jesus responds, "My kingdom is not of this world. If my kingdom were of this world, my servants would have been fighting, that I might not be delivered over to the Jews. But my kingdom is not from the world" (John 18:36). If Jesus's followers

2 Here I use the term *powers* as the New Testament writers do: to refer to demonic beings.

3 Paul clearly has demonic powers in mind here when he mentions the "rulers of this age." The earthly rulers who put Jesus to death—Pilate and the chief priests—were relatively unconcerned by his resurrection since it did nothing in the short term to upset their political power.

are not fighting, Satan's kingdom is very much of this world, and his followers are fighting. They've come to torture and kill. They have no other way to maintain power.

It's here that we see the contrast at its clearest: Jesus's kingdom has no need to meet force with force, despite the legions of angels at his disposal (Matt. 26:53). He is willing to let Satan's agents torment, overpower, and execute him because he's confident that he will be vindicated by God and resurrected. He knows God will use this victory to end Satan's empire of death and suffering altogether.

The victory Jesus wins over Satan is immediate, and it sets his followers free from Satan's slavery. Before the resurrection, Peter denies Jesus out of fear. After the resurrection, he and the other apostles find courage to stand in the face of persecution (see Acts 4:1–22). Jesus's resurrection made it clear that they have nothing left to dread. They've seen the resurrected Christ, so they now know that one day they too will be raised from the dead.

Following Jesus in His Sufferings

Church history tells us that this hope led most of the apostles to submit to martyrdom. We tend to imagine that Jesus suffered so that we wouldn't have to. In one sense, of course, that's true. We will not suffer under God's wrath. But the Scriptures also indicate Jesus died so that we might also submit to suffering and death with him and afterward may enter with him into glory. The cross is not just the means of God's goodness to us; it's the *pattern* of his goodness to us. Suffering comes before lasting glory; Calvary comes before Easter. Satan came for Jesus, and he will also come for us. When he does, God may choose to lead us through Satan's terrors rather than around them, through even death itself. But we know with certainty we will make it out the other side.

If we refuse to share in Christ's sufferings, we have no hope of eternal life. Paul tells us we are "heirs of God and fellow heirs with Christ, *provided we suffer with him* in order that we may also be glorified with him" (Rom. 8:17). Similarly, Hebrews encourages its suffering readers that "we have come to share in Christ, *if indeed we hold our original confidence firm*" (Heb. 3:14). And Peter tells us, "But rejoice insofar as you share Christ's sufferings, that you may also rejoice and be glad when his glory is revealed" (1 Pet. 4:13).

To return to the scriptural image we saw earlier in this chapter, we have been freed from slavery, but our exodus still involves a difficult journey home. As God called Israel to journey out of the "groaning" (Ex. 2:24) of slavery to be his "firstborn son" (Ex. 4:22), so we find ourselves and God's creation on a difficult journey. Paul reminds us:

> Creation itself will be set free from its bondage to corruption and obtain the freedom of the glory of the children of God. For we know that the whole creation has been groaning together in the pains of childbirth until now. And not only creation, but we ourselves, who have the firstfruits of the Spirit, groan inwardly as we wait eagerly for adoption as sons, the redemption of our bodies." (Rom. 8:21–23)

Do you see the many parallels Paul draws with the exodus in this passage? We "groan" like Israel in bondage; we are delivered, like Israel, from the "bondage" of slavery; we are adopted, like Israel, as God's children. Like Israel, we must take a difficult journey as we "wait eagerly for [our] adoption as sons" to be complete.

This is what many evangelicals refer to as the "already/not yet" aspect of our salvation. Our salvation is secure from the moment our faith in Jesus awakens, but it's not fully accomplished until our journey is complete. Our adoption has been accomplished and our status as God's children is secure (see Rom. 8:15), but we haven't yet set foot in our new home. We're still waiting for our adoption to come to its full completion (see Rom. 8:23).

The theme of our Christian life as a journey to freedom—as a second Exodus—is repeated throughout the New Testament:

- Jesus chooses the Passover (John 13), the celebration of the original exodus (Ex. 12), as the time for his crucifixion, and tells the disciples that they will follow him on a difficult road to a place he has prepared for them (John 13:36; 14:3).
- The author of Hebrews warns his suffering readers not to harden their hearts and turn back as their forefathers did in the wilderness (Heb. 3:7–11).
- Peter speaks of our waiting for a promised land: "But according to his promise we are waiting for new heavens and a new earth in which righteousness dwells" (2 Pet. 3:13).[4]

Seeing the Christian life as a journey out of slavery will help us understand why the New Testament insists we must first follow Christ through his sufferings before we enter his glory. It will also help us avoid a theology of salvation by our own "works of suffering." As Israel was redeemed from slavery by God's power alone (Deut. 7:6–7), so it is Christ alone who has redeemed us from our slavery. As it was God's power alone that sustained the children

4 In this passage, Peter is referencing Isa. 65:17, which speaks of the creation of "new heavens and a new earth." Isaiah clearly has God's promised land in mind, since he locates the blessing of this new heavens and new earth in Israel in the following verses: "I create Jerusalem to be a joy, and her people to be a gladness. I will rejoice in Jerusalem and be glad in my people" (Isa. 65:18–19).

of Israel through the wilderness, so it is Christ's power alone that sustains us on our pilgrimage. Although our suffering plays no role in *earning* our freedom, all who have genuine faith in Christ will ultimately endure the difficulties they encounter along the way. My friend Sadiq continues following Christ through persecution because he trusts where Christ is leading him.

I said in chapter 1 that questions of theodicy would mostly be sidenotes throughout this book, but let's glance at them briefly here. Why, after setting us free from sin, does God insist on bringing us to glory through suffering? Why doesn't he transport us there immediately?

It may help us to remember that we were the ones who sold ourselves into Satan's grasp in the first place. God has decided not to simply bypass those choices. Tim Keller explains, "God's plan works *through* our choices, not around or despite them."[5] He is a living God who meets us in the messiness of human history, not a genie who snaps his fingers and whisks our problems away every time history takes a wrong turn or we make a wrong choice. Just as he didn't instantly transport the children of Israel out of Egypt and across the desert, so he doesn't transport us instantly from our fallen bodies to glory. Instead, he faithfully upholds us on our painful journey to the place where finally our bodies die and we cross over Jordan to the land of promise.

Put simply, God doesn't *remove* the consequences of our evil choices; he works through them to *redeem* us. Paul writes:

> We know that our old self was crucified with him in order that the body of sin might be brought to nothing, so that we would

5 Timothy Keller, *Walking with God Through Pain and Suffering* (Hodder & Stoughton, 2015), 140, emphasis original.

> no longer be enslaved to sin. . . . Now if we have died with Christ, we believe that we will also live with him. . . . For the death he died he died to sin, once for all, but the life he lives he lives to God. So you also must consider yourselves dead to sin and alive to God in Christ Jesus. (Rom. 6:6–11)

> For if you live according to the flesh you will die, but if by the Spirit you put to death the deeds of the body, you will live. (Rom. 8:13)

In other words, the "old self" has died, and God uses the painful process of helping us recognize this ("consider yourselves dead to sin") to renew our character ("put to death the deeds of the body"). This is what the Reformers and Puritans referred to as the mortification of sin.[6]

But the mortification of sin isn't the only difficult experience we walk through on the way to our new life. Instead, walking through suffering and death itself is part of our journey. Paul also tells us, "So it is with the resurrection of the dead. What is sown is perishable; what is raised is imperishable. It is sown in dishonor; it is raised in glory. It is sown in weakness; it is raised in power. It is sown a natural body; it is raised a spiritual body" (1 Cor. 15:42–44). Our literal, bodily death leads to our literal, bodily resurrection. Suffering and death are part of the road to resurrection and renewal, and we must pass through them to reach the promised land. "Blessed are the dead who die in the Lord from now on," because, having passed through suffering and death with Christ, they have journeyed beyond the power and fear of death.

6 John Owen, *The Mortification of Sin* (1656; repr., Reformed Church Publications, 2015).

They are fully beyond Satan's afflictions at last, and "they may rest from their labors" (Rev. 14:13).

A Suffering Priesthood

When God calls us to follow him on a difficult journey, he isn't merely interested in setting us free; he wants us to call others out of slavery along the way. As we do, we'll suffer Satan's rage. He'll use suffering to terrify and discourage us, but standing firm is our only option. Loving others enough to suffer for them is a fundamental part of what it means to be dead to sin and alive to God.[7]

We can't afford to miss the significance of the ministry we have been given, because it restores humanity to the priestly role God always intended for us. I realize "priestly ministry" sounds like a technical, theologically loaded phrase, but its meaning is quite simple. It means we have the privilege and responsibility of ushering creation—including our fellow image bearers—into God's presence. In the beginning, God called Adam and Eve to rule as priests and to reflect God's image and presence to all creation.[8] When Adam and Eve fell and were exiled from God's presence, he called Israel

7 John writes, "Love is from God, and whoever loves has been born of God. . . . In this is love, not that we have loved God but that he loved us and sent his Son to be the propitiation for our sins. Beloved, if God so loved us, we also ought to love one another" (1 John 4:7–11). The new life we have been born into in God, then, necessarily involves loving others as God loves and being willing to endure loss for them.

8 Thus, Eden is a portrayed as a sanctuary (e.g., Isa. 51:3; Ezek. 28:13). Adam's "working" and "guarding" (Gen. 2:15) the garden are only reflected elsewhere in God's calling of the priests (Num. 3:7–8; 8:25–26; 18:5–7); the gold crown (Ex. 29:6; 30:30) and ephod (Ex. 28:6–14) and the onyx shoulder pieces (Ex. 28:9–11) of the priestly garments are reminiscent of the gold and onyx of Eden (Gen. 2:12). All nine precious stones mentioned of Ezekiel's glorious being (Ezek. 28:13) in Eden are found on the high priest's ephod (Ex. 28:17–20) and are sometimes mentioned in the exact same order as the rows of precious stones in the ephod ("beryl . . . onyx . . . jasper"), etc. For more, see David Schrock, *The Royal Priesthood and the Glory of God* (Crossway, 2022).

to be a "kingdom of priests" (Ex. 19:6) and draw the nations to him (e.g., Gen. 12:3). But Israel, too, was corrupted by sin and eventually found itself exiled from the presence it was meant to usher the nations into.

Adam and Israel both failed as priests. Thankfully, the mantle was picked up and fulfilled in Christ, and Christ's church was established as a new "royal priesthood" (1 Pet. 2:9) to usher the nations into God's presence. The church's missionary calling is part of her priestly calling. Indeed, the Great Commission is a recapitulation of God's first command to Adam and Eve to multiply and establish their priestly dominion over the earth (Gen. 1:28). And Paul describes his missionary work as a "priestly service of the gospel of God, so that the offering of the Gentiles may be acceptable, sanctified by the Holy Spirit" (Rom. 15:16).[9]

Please understand, I'm not trying to replace the "priesthood of all believers" with a "priesthood of only missionaries." Rather, I'm arguing that part of the priestly task has always been to mediate God's presence to creation, and especially to fallen humanity. Missionary efforts play one of many crucial roles in this task. But what does it mean for the missionary endeavor to be part of the church's priestly vocation? How do we usher the nations into God's presence?

We can begin to understand our priestly calling by looking at Christ's. Specifically, Jesus's priestly calling centered around his offering of himself as a sacrifice to usher us into God's presence. Hebrews tells us that "Christ . . . as a high priest . . . entered once for all into the holy places . . . by means of his own blood . . . [to]

9 See also 1 Cor. 9:13–14, where Paul compares his missionary work with the Old Testament priesthood.

purify our conscience from dead works to serve the living God" (Heb. 9:11–14).

Our priestly ministry also involves offering ourselves as a sacrifice to God. Paul tells the Romans, "Present your bodies as a living sacrifice, holy and acceptable to God, which is your spiritual service of worship" (Rom. 12:1, my translation). "Spiritual service of worship," if we understand the scriptural connotations of the phrase, can only be priestly service.[10] Similarly, Peter writes, "As you come to him, a living stone rejected by men . . . you yourselves like living stones are being built up as a spiritual house, to be a holy priesthood, to offer spiritual sacrifices acceptable to God through Jesus Christ" (1 Pet. 2:4–5).

Again, Peter links the priesthood to offering "spiritual sacrifices" and, specifically, the sacrifice of being "rejected by men" as Christ was (cf. Ps. 118:22; Isa. 53:3; Matt. 21:42). And just as Jesus's priestly sacrifice was offered for our sake, so our sacrifices to God are offered for the sake of others. Notice how Paul describes being imprisoned for preaching the gospel:

> Even if I am to be poured out as a drink offering upon the sacrificial offering of your faith, I am glad and rejoice with you all. (Phil. 2:17)

> For I am already being poured out as a drink offering, and the time of my departure has come. (2 Tim. 4:6)

10 In the Old Testament, the primary service of the priest is to help people bring their sacrifices to God. The vast majority of acts described in the Old Testament as "worship" of God involve the offering of sacrifices (e.g., Gen. 22:5; Deut. 12:3–6; 12:31, 26:10; Josh. 22:25–26; 1 Sam. 1:3, 15:25; 2 Sam. 15:8–12; 2 Kings 18:22; 1 Chron. 16:29; 2 Chron. 32:12; Isa. 19:21, 36:7). In many other cases, sacrifice is implied in "worship" since worship is seen as specifically being offered in the temple or in Israel's feasts, which involved sacrifice (e.g., Ezra 6:20–22; Pss. 96:8–9; 99:9).

> Now I rejoice in my sufferings for your sake, and in my flesh I am filling up what is lacking in Christ's afflictions for the sake of his body, that is, the church. (Col. 1:24)

Again and again, our ministry as Christians, our priestly service, involves following Christ by offering ourselves as a sacrifice to God as we suffer for the sake of others.

You could be forgiven if you're starting to feel nervous. The idea that we offer ourselves as a sacrifice to God for the sake of his people seems to come perilously close to stealing for ourselves a part of Christ's glory as Savior of the world. But I'm not wandering outside of Christian orthodoxy. Martin Luther, the greatest historical proponent of the priesthood of all believers, wrote, "Men universally consider the title of priest glorious and honorable; it is acceptable to everyone. But the duties and the sacrifice of the office are rarely accepted. . . . The Christian priesthood costs life, property, honor, friends, and all worldly things."[11]

John Piper's summary of Romanian pastor Joseph Tson's teaching is helpful: "Christ's suffering is for *propitiation*; our suffering is for *propagation*."[12] As God used Christ's sufferings to purchase people's freedom from their slavery to sin and Satan, he now works through our sufferings to let people know they can be free. Thus, Paul writes:

> But thanks be to God, who in Christ always leads us in triumphal procession, and through us spreads the fragrance of the knowledge of him everywhere. For we are the aroma of Christ to

11 Martin Luther, "First Sunday after Epiphany," in *Luther's Epistle Sermons: Epiphany, Easter, and Pentecost*, trans. John Nicholas Lenker (The Luther Press, 1909), 9.

12 John Piper, *Filling Up the Afflictions of Christ: The Cost of Bringing the Gospel to the Nations in the Lives of William Tyndale, Adoniram Judson, and John Paton* (Crossway, 2009), 15, emphasis original.

> God among those who are being saved and among those who are perishing, to one a fragrance from death to death, to the other a fragrance from life to life. (2 Cor. 2:14–16)

Here again we have the language of sacrifice ("fragrance"[13] and "aroma"[14]), and the result is that the knowledge of God is spread everywhere, leading from "life to life"—from Jesus's resurrected life to new life for "those who are being saved."

It will be easier to understand why the New Testament writers discuss offering ourselves as a "sacrifice" if we stop thinking of sacrifice in vague, theological terms. We need to realize how everything discussed in chapter 2 about the ways Satan brings suffering and persecution on believers was already happening in the lives of the apostles when they wrote the New Testament. The apostles' priestly ministry took place in a world where Satan and the powers were very active. As the apostles called people to God, Satan responded predictably by inciting beatings, imprisonment, and martyrdom.

This doesn't mean the apostles thought that only obvious sufferings were acceptable sacrifices to God. God apportions different sufferings to each of us. If God allowed for Paul to be killed ("poured out as a drink offering upon the sacrificial offering of your faith," Phil. 2:17), then the far less costly financial gift that his readers gave him was still a "fragrant offering, a sacrifice acceptable and pleasing to God" (Phil. 4:18). All Christians have sacrifices to offer God as we spread the knowledge of him in different places, and we all face different hardships along the way as we offer those sacrifices.

13 See Eph. 5:2; Phil. 4:18.

14 See Ex. 29:18, 25; Lev. 1:9–17; Num. 15:3; etc.

But how does the sacrifice of our suffering bring people to know God? Let's look at how the Scriptures describe the role of suffering in our lives and ministries. As we do, we'll follow the specific focuses of this book and pay special attention to the ways in which missionary suffering brings the nations to the knowledge of Christ.

The Price of Ministry

Paul writes to the Philippians, "My desire is to depart and be with Christ, for that is far better. But to remain in the flesh is more necessary on your account. Convinced of this, I know that I will remain and continue with you all, for your progress and joy in the faith" (Phil. 1:23–25).

Paul longs for his final rest and glory with Christ. He has grown weary of this fallen world. But he also knows he can't minister to the Philippians if he "departs" the world to be with Christ, so he sees his suffering as worthwhile. Our suffering is worthwhile, too, as it's the price we pay for remaining and doing ministry in this fallen world.

We instinctively understand how Paul's towering list of sufferings played a role in God's plan, but we tend to have less hope for our own sufferings. After all, in light of Paul being beaten, imprisoned, shipwrecked, stoned, and finally martyred, our own sufferings don't seem to merit much mention. What's more, Paul's sufferings were often caused by people who opposed his ministry. In contrast, our own sufferings seem more pedestrian, more "ordinary." We suffer from loneliness, interpersonal conflict, sickness, exhaustion, and the slow decay of our bodies. But these sufferings, too, if we offer them to God, are a sacrifice through which God acts to redeem the world. They're the price tag attached to being in the world so that we can minister to the world.

All our sufferings—both large and small—can be offered as sacrifices to God. As Christ's own sufferings included not only dying so that others might live but also leaving his heavenly glory behind and becoming poor so that others "by his poverty might become rich" (2 Cor. 8:9), so, too, we can suffer for Christ not only by dying but also by being "unknown," "sorrowful," and "poor, yet making many rich" (2 Cor. 6:9–10). The New Testament uses language of sacrifice to describe not only the martyrdom of believers (Phil. 2:17; 2 Tim. 4:6) but also their imprisonment (Col. 1:24), rejection (Heb. 13:13–15),[15] and sharing of their belongings (Phil. 4:18). Your sufferings, too—however large or small they may be—will play a part in the working out of Christ's victory. Each sorrow you suffer, each disappointment, grief, rejection, bereavement, separation, sickness, or pain is a specific price that you pay for living in this dark and broken world in which Christ has called you to be a light (Matt. 5:16).

Missionaries, you may pay a steeper price by being among the people you minister to. But the same is true for you—whatever persecution you may face or suffering you may endure as a result of your ministry is given to God as a sacrifice: distance from family, cultural disorientation, persecution, unfamiliar diseases, long years of language learning, living in impoverished or unsafe

15 In Hebrews 13:15, "sacrifice of praise" (*thusian aineseōs*) is a reference to Old Testament thank offerings in Lev. 7:12–15. Thus, the author of Hebrews is telling his readers to follow Jesus "outside the camp" (Heb. 13:13) and to offer "a thank offering, the fruit of lips that confess [*homologeō*] his name" (Heb. 13:15, my translation). In the context of a letter encouraging suffering believers to "hold fast our confession [*homologia*]" (Heb. 4:14; cf. 10:23), Hebrews 13:15 is telling believers that as a thank offering, they must endure whatever suffering might follow from confessing their faith. "Sharing," in Hebrews 13:16, is to be understood in light of going outside the camp to pursue a city that is to come (Heb. 13:13–14). The Greek word here, *koinōnia*, is found in only one other place in Hebrews, where it speaks not of sharing material goods but of being partners with those who are being persecuted (Heb. 10:33).

circumstances. It's all part of the price tag for being among the people you minister to.

A few months ago, my wife, Kim, realized that a close friend was stealing from her. It was a devastating discovery because she dearly loved this friend. And then, that very night, in an unrelated incident, our house was robbed and everything of value was taken. The robbery came only two weeks after a neighbor was stabbed to death in his sleep by thieves, so it was concerning that the thieves had clearly cut their way through a screen door in one room with one of the large knives that local men carry. What would have happened if we'd been in the room they robbed? About a week later, police found most of our belongings but said they couldn't return them until we paid an enormous sum they claimed to owe their informant.

First stolen from by a friend, then robbed at night, and finally extorted by the police, we struggled to trust anyone around us. And then Kim said softly, "This is why we came here, isn't it? To speak Christ's message to people who steal and lie because they don't know him?"

There's nothing particularly impressive about what Kim and I went through. We weren't robbed by angry extremists who hated our message. We took no courageous stands for Christ during the robbery. We didn't even know it was happening! And we got almost everything back. Still, we were able to offer this difficulty and others like it to God. If we continue to do so willingly, we know he will be pleased with our sacrifice. Whether the price you pay to be among those you minister to seems impressive or not, it's a sacrifice that you can offer to God.

Enacting Christ's Victory

There is another way that God uses our sufferings to minister to others. He uses the hardships that we endure, both "ordinary" and ministry-related, to reveal the truth of the gospel to people around us. Paul writes to the Corinthians:

> We are afflicted in every way, but not crushed; perplexed, but not driven to despair; persecuted, but not forsaken; struck down, but not destroyed; always carrying in the body the death of Jesus, so that the life of Jesus also may be manifested in our bodies. For we who live are always being given over to death for Jesus' sake, so that the life of Jesus also may be manifested in our mortal flesh. So death is at work in us, but life in you. . . . For it is all for your sake. (2 Cor. 4:8–15)

In chapter 2, we saw that Christ's sufferings were a sort of dark street theater intended by both Roman and demonic authorities to intimidate people. But there is another, deeper sense in which the sufferings of God's people serve as a theater. As the Corinthians see Paul's suffering, they also see supernatural strength sustaining him. God's resurrection power is "manifested" in the way he is not crushed, driven to despair, forsaken, or destroyed (2 Cor. 4:8–9). Paul is enacting the gospel message before their eyes, giving them visible evidence of a God who can raise both Christ and them from the dead. That's why, as we saw above, Paul can say elsewhere that his sufferings give off the "aroma of Christ" and act as a "fragrance from *life to life*." He wants us to know that his sufferings carry an aroma of Christ's resurrection life that is strong enough to lead to knowledge of God and new life "among those who are being saved" (2 Cor. 2:14–16).

Paul has something similar in mind when he says God "exhibited" his sufferings as a "spectacle to the world" (1 Cor. 4:9).[16]

16 The Greek word *apedeichen* is curiously translated "exhibited" here in the ESV, leaving Paul claiming that he has been "exhibited" as a "spectacle." This translation may leave

Paul isn't feeling sorry for himself and complaining that God made his life into a bizarre sideshow of suffering. Instead, the Greek word *theatron* that the ESV renders "spectacle" is translated as "theater" in its other two New Testament occurrences (Acts 19:29, 31). Paul's point, then, is that his sufferings, which the Corinthians have seen as a sign of weakness and foolishness (e.g., 1 Cor. 1:18–2:5; 4:10–13), are actually a theater through which God is putting the wisdom and power of the cross on display (1 Cor. 1:24). He mentions his sufferings not to shock the Corinthians but to remind them to imitate him and his "ways in Christ" and not continue in their arrogant disdain of his weakness (1 Cor. 4:16–18).

Again, this display of God's resurrection power happens not only in sufferings like persecution that are obviously "spiritual" or ministry-related but also in the daily, "ordinary" sufferings. Paul's thorn in the flesh is simply a physical ailment, yet he tells the Corinthians that Christ's resurrection power is revealed and released through it:

> Three times I pleaded with the Lord about this, that it should leave me. But he said to me, "My grace is sufficient for you, for my power is made perfect in weakness." Therefore I will boast all the more gladly of my weaknesses, so that the power of Christ may rest upon me. (2 Cor. 12:8–9)

How important is this in ministry, especially on the mission field? If you have understood the previous chapter, you'll realize why the

---

most English-speaking readers imagining that God's intent is to shock people. But in its other uses, *apedeichen* is simply rendered "attested" (Acts 2:22), "prove" (Acts 25:7), and "proclaiming" (2 Thess. 2:4).

revelation of God's resurrection power in our sufferings is essential. It is through "fear of death" (Heb. 2:15) that Satan enslaves and blinds people. The display of God's resurrection power in our sufferings sets them free from this fear. Our sufferings, like Paul's, are ultimately "for [the] sake" of others (2 Cor. 4:15) because they allow us not only to *tell* people the truth of the gospel but also to *show* them that truth.

Remember our friend Sadiq at the start of this chapter? As the years have passed, people in Sadiq's city who wanted to learn more about Christ have often sought him out. Why? Because his willingness to suffer for the sake of Christ has consistently demonstrated the value and power of Christ in his life. Those of us who serve as missionaries can trust that God will use our sufferings in the same way. We go overseas not only declaring the gospel but also demonstrating and enacting its power. This is how mission fields are won.

Suffering as More Than Just an Individual Affair

So far, as I have explained the role of suffering in the Christian life, I have paid little attention to the ways God uses it to grow our individual character. This isn't because I don't think God uses suffering to grow us as individuals, but because the heavy emphasis of Scripture is on us sharing in Christ's sufferings. Christ had no personal needs or character shortcomings to address when he suffered. His sufferings were for the sake of others. And while we may experience personal growth through our sufferings, Scripture focuses on the way we follow Christ in suffering for the sake of others.

When the Gentiles seek to speak to Jesus before his sufferings, Jesus says:

> Truly, truly, I say to you, unless a grain of wheat falls into the earth and dies, it remains alone; but if it dies, it bears much fruit. . . . Now is my soul troubled. And what shall I say? "Father, save me from this hour"? But for this purpose I have come to this hour. Father, glorify your name. . . . Now will the ruler of this world be cast out. And I, when I am lifted up from the earth, will draw all people to myself. (John 12:24–32)

This passage is especially relevant to the missionary task. Jesus indicates that when he is crucified, he will succeed in defeating Satan and draw not only Jews but also Gentiles to himself. He wants his disciples to realize that their suffering will also lead others to know the Father. Just a few days later, Jesus says, "I am the true vine, and my Father is the vinedresser. Every branch in me that does not bear fruit he takes away, and every branch that does bear fruit he prunes, that it may bear more fruit" (John 15:1–2). Modern preaching usually assumes that "pruning" here is a metaphor for trials that result in personal character growth. This interpretation is unlikely because it overlooks the undeniable parallels between John 12:24–32 and John 15:1–2. Both show the fatal lifting of something from a plant, followed by an excess of fruit. And both suggest a frightful alternative to this painful process: The seed will remain alone and fail in its purpose (John 12:24), and the branches will be taken away and burned (John 15:6).

In context, when Jesus tells his disciples that every branch that bears fruit will be pruned and bear more fruit, he is not telling them that God will use suffering to grow their character (though he may). Jesus is telling his apostles that they, like him, will suffer as part of their ministry and that their suffering, and even death, will lead to more fruit. It becomes even clearer that this is what Jesus is talking about when, just a few verses later, he tells his disciples they must be ready to suffer and die for the sake of others:[17]

> This is my commandment, that you love one another as I have loved you. Greater love has no one than this, that someone lay down his life for his friends. . . . If the world hates you, know that it has hated me before it hated you. . . . If they persecuted me, they will also persecute you. (John 15:12–13, 18–20)

We should certainly try to learn what we can from our suffering, but do you see what we will do if we make personal character growth our primary focus? We will privatize our suffering, imagining it was more for our own sake than for that of the wider church. We will begin to think, "If I'm suffering, then there must be something in it for me." But in the New Testament, suffering is never a private affair. Each member's suffering affects the wider body. Paul says, "If one member suffers, all suffer together" (1 Cor. 12:26), and each member suffers primarily for the sake of the wider body. Paul writes from prison that he is "filling up what is lacking in Christ's afflictions *for the sake of his body, that is, the church*" (Col. 1:24) and that he endures "everything *for the sake of the elect*" (2 Tim. 2:10). In a purely pragmatic sense, it is undeniable that he's suffering for the sake of the churches. After all, Paul is in prison because he preached to them.

17 Indeed, it would have been more clear to John's early Jewish readers that this is what Jesus had in mind. The parable of a vine branch being pruned and bearing fruit would have reminded them of Isaiah's branch that comes out of a stump to "bear fruit" (Isa. 11:1). Again, the parallel is obviously intended, and New Testament writers did not see Isaiah's prophecy as a promise that suffering would lead to character growth but as a reference to the salvation Christ brought to sinners through his suffering and resurrection (e.g., Rom. 15:12).

Our own sufferings, too, will often be primarily for the sake of others. If we fail to recognize this, we may be unable to respond wisely and appropriately when suffering comes. Arguing that people suffer only because God has something to teach them assumes that God lets Christians suffer only to correct their immaturity or sin. This veers dangerously close to the twisted thinking of Job's friends. Pastor Blake Glosson explains that this thinking places

> an unnecessary yoke on the back of the sufferer. It adds guilt if she hasn't "figured out God's lesson" yet, and it can imply that she's at fault for her suffering: "Maybe if you didn't idolize being a mother, God wouldn't have allowed your miscarriage . . ." The Bible teaches that all suffering is a result of sin (Rom. 5:12) but all suffering is not a consequence of personal sin. To blame someone's suffering on his sin is often presumptuous, usually unhelpful, and always simplistic.[18]

Why not believe instead that both our suffering and the suffering of other Christians is simply part of the price tag of ministering in a fallen world? Why not acknowledge that God uses our suffering to demonstrate his power to those around us? We don't need to shoot the wounded by accusing them of immaturity. Nor do we need to downplay the terrible extent of their suffering by imagining that whatever gains we observe in others' character—which sometimes may be quite marginal (if they are already mature)—are all that is needed to make their suffering worthwhile.

18 Blake Glosson, "In Suffering, God Isn't (Simply) Teaching You a Lesson," The Gospel Coalition, January 18, 2023, https://www.thegospelcoalition.org.

We can briefly pause here again to glance at questions of theodicy. Why does God ask us to suffer for the sake of others? Could a good God ask this of us?

I suppose God could have created each of us on a private planet where we were entirely unaffected by the sins and weaknesses of others. But what we have found so far suggests that fixating on such questions may say more about our character than God's. We didn't protest much when Christ the innocent suffered on our behalf. Now if we—who were complicit in handing the world over to Satan and the powers and in their filling the world with suffering—are asked to suffer for the sake of others, shouldn't we respond with an enthusiastic *yes*? Paul, who suffered so much in his ministry, does not feel ill-used by God because of his suffering for the churches. Rather, he says, "I will most gladly spend and be spent for your souls" (2 Cor. 12:15).

He wastes no time wondering whether it is fair that he must suffer for their sake. Paul can no longer think that way. He is a man transformed by the love of Christ, and Christ's love controls him so that he can no longer fixate on his own well-being (2 Cor. 5:15). He loves his churches like his own children (1 Cor. 4:15), and his missionary heart is glad to suffer if he can benefit the people he loves, even though it would be better for him personally to leave this tired world.

Conclusion

In the previous chapter, we saw that Satan and the powers took dominion over the earth from humanity, filling the world with pain and destruction and using the fear of death to enslave people. We can now add more to this story. In this chapter, we can draw several conclusions from what we have seen:

- Rather than overpowering Satan and the powers to free us, Jesus entrusted himself to God and submitted himself to be overpowered and murdered by them.
- God responded to Jesus's sacrifice by raising him from the dead and granting eternal life to all who trust him.
- The hope of this resurrection sets us free from the fear of suffering and death, which Satan used to enslave us.
- Jesus freed us from slavery and now calls us to follow him through a suffering world (and death itself) to a promised land beyond the reach of sin and suffering.
- Our sufferings as we follow Jesus on this journey are, like Jesus's own sufferings, a sacrifice offered to God for the sake of others.
- Whereas Jesus's sacrifice was offered as a *propitiation* for sin, ours is offered to accomplish the *proclamation* of the gospel.
- We offer this suffering sacrifice, in part, simply as the price of remaining in this fallen world, where we can proclaim the gospel to others.
- A missionary's presence among the unreached of this world—and whatever sufferings might attend it—is a sacrifice that allows him or her to call lost people to Christ.
- God uses his people's sufferings in this world as a theater to re-enact the gospel story and demonstrate his resurrection power sustaining us, so that many can believe in the resurrection and be set free from their slavery to fear.

At this point, perhaps we can begin to see how following the emphases of Scripture rather than theodicy leads to a clearer, more satisfying way of addressing theodicy's troubling questions. But we haven't finished yet.

As I suggested in chapter 1, a scriptural theology of suffering is only one facet of a larger theology of joy. I've spoken about the difficulties of the journey, but so far I've only hinted at the promised land (i.e., the joy) that we are heading toward. It is by far the most significant and wonderful part of the story, and we spend the next chapter exploring it.

4

The Promised Land

And they continue to this day to desire to shed my blood. But of these things I have no care; for I know and am persuaded that they who endure shall receive a reward from our Savior, and . . . shall be able to glory, and . . . shall receive the "crown of life."

ATHANASIUS
To the Bishops of Egypt and Libya

SUFFERING IS PART of the journey, but journeys don't last forever. They exist to take us somewhere. Our sufferings won't last forever either, but joy will. Joy is the great goal that finally brings God's purposes for suffering together. One day our exodus will be over and we will find ourselves in the promised land.

During my loneliest years of missionary service, the danger for me was to think of myself as a sort of tragic hero. "Perhaps I'm suffering for the sake of others," I told myself. "That's all well and good for them, and I'm glad there's a greater good being accomplished. But is it basically just hard luck for me? Or will I gain something through all the difficulty?" Finding answers to these questions sustained me during the most difficult stretches of my missionary career.

Of course, other missionaries have endured far greater difficulties than I have. In such cases, the knowledge that God rewards and redeems our suffering is even more vital. I was single when I first left for the field, and the Sunday when my church commissioned me to go overseas, a family with six children was commissioned alongside me. The father, a wonderful man named Chris, died overseas two years later, leaving behind his wife and children. On the evening of his death, his wife, Michelle, wrote to ask for prayer for the people her family had been sent to. She specifically asked that the people they were ministering to "would know the ONE TRUE GOD, Sovereign over all spirits, the One who has known Chris from when he was knit together in his mother's womb to this evening when he received his heavenly reward."[1]

In the wake of unspeakable loss, the knowledge of Chris's reward sustained Michelle. Can you imagine what might have happened to her faith if she imagined that God viewed her husband's passing as unfortunate collateral damage and had no intention of redeeming it? Whatever we lose, and especially when we face great loss, the hope of a reward will sustain us too.

A Theology of Reward

Though I suggested in the previous chapter that our sufferings will often be primarily for the sake of others, that doesn't mean we are somehow treated unfairly. Jesus suffered primarily for our sake, but he was still richly rewarded, and the same will be true for us.

1 Michelle Gennaro-Lapp, *Worst Case Scenario: Finding Overwhelming Rescue in the Promises of God* (Xulon, 2023), 329.

If we follow Christ in his sufferings, God will make sure the difficulty we bear is worth it to us in the end. He will not allow us to suffer as tragic heroes who neither reap a reward nor see any fruit. He will make sure that our suffering is rewarded. We are "heirs of God and fellow heirs with Christ, provided we suffer with him in order that we may also be glorified with him" (Rom. 8:17). Who gains this great reward? Who ultimately shares Christ's inheritance? Who inherits the promised land? All of us who suffer with Jesus.

Again, this promise is not specific to missionaries or those who suffer in unusual ways. It's a promise given for all who bear the sufferings of this life for Jesus, in ways great and small, as he leads them to the promised land. Jonathan Edwards writes, "Those who are willing thus to spend their lives as a journey towards heaven may have heaven."[2] God is at work in our sufferings, but that's only half the story. It would be more accurate to say that God is working to redeem our sufferings and bring us through them to everlasting glory.

As missionaries go to disciple the unreached, we must cling to the hope of the promised land. When new churches suffer, we must teach them to hold fast to God's promises. Encouraging them to do so is a fundamental part of preaching the gospel, especially in persecuted settings. Writing to persecuted Christians, the author of Hebrews says, "We are not of those who shrink back and are destroyed, but of those who have faith and preserve their souls" (Heb. 10:39). He continues by reminding them that "without faith it is impossible to please him, for whoever would draw near to God must believe that he exists and that he rewards those who seek him" (Heb. 11:6). Do you understand what the author of Hebrews is

2 Jonathan Edwards, "The Christian Pilgrim, Or, The True Christian's Life a Journey Toward Heaven," in *The Works of Jonathan Edwards*, vol. 1 (London: Westley and Davis, 1835), 246.

saying? The hope of a reward is an indispensable part of biblical faith. Without this hope people are likely to "shrink back and [be] destroyed." Therefore, the author wants us to look past death to the reward of our glorious resurrection.

That's why the "hall of faith" in Hebrews 11 pays special attention to how Old Testament saints looked past death to their future reward. For instance, Abraham believed that God would give him descendants though he was "as good as dead" (Heb. 11:12), and that God would raise Isaac from the dead (Heb. 11:19). Isaac believed that blessing his sons "invoked future blessings" after he died (Heb. 11:20). Jacob believed that his descendants would be blessed after he died (Heb. 11:21), and Joseph believed in the future exodus of his people (Heb. 11:22). The entire "hall of faith" is leading to an exhortation to trust that God will raise us from the dead, just as he did with Jesus. Therefore, the author says:

> Let us run with endurance the race that is set before us, looking to Jesus, the founder and perfecter of our faith, who for the joy that was set before him endured the cross, despising the shame, and is seated at the right hand of the throne of God. Consider him who endured from sinners such hostility against himself, so that you may not grow weary or fainthearted. In your struggle against sin you have not yet resisted to the point of shedding your blood. (Heb. 12:1–4)

The author of Hebrews wants his readers to have faith to endure, even if they face martyrdom as Jesus did, looking past death to their final reward.

Certainly, we may have glimpses of our reward along the way. God gives miraculous deliverances and seasons of great blessing even in this life, and I don't want to undervalue those for a moment. Hebrews tells us that through faith, God's people have "conquered kingdoms, enforced justice, obtained promises, stopped the mouths of lions, quenched the power of fire, escaped the edge of the sword, were made strong out of weakness, became mighty in war, put foreign armies to flight. Women received back their dead by resurrection" (Heb. 11:33–35).

But there are also great tragedies that befall God's people in this life. The author continues:

> Some were tortured, refusing to accept release, so that they might rise again to a better life. Others suffered mocking and flogging, and even chains and imprisonment. They were stoned, they were sawn in two, they were killed with the sword. They went about in skins of sheep and goats, destitute, afflicted, mistreated—of whom the world was not worthy—wandering about in deserts and mountains, and in dens and caves of the earth. (Heb. 11:35–38)

Rewards in this life are as uncertain as they are temporary. While they may serve as foretastes of our final reward, they can never compare with it. Chinese pastor San Shou explains, "Christians know they might lose everything, or they might gain everything. Both are temporary. But God gives what the world cannot give: eternal life."[3]

Without such a hope, how can churches in persecuted areas survive? We can endure our journey through the desert only by looking forward to the promised land. For the joy set before us, we endure

3 San Shou, "Our Hope," in *Faith in the Wilderness: Words of Exhortation from the Chinese Church*, ed. Hannah Nation and Simon Liu (Lexham, 2022), 128.

suffering just as Christ did. Missionaries who don't believe that eternal joy awaits them will be unable to endure the sufferings of their ministry over the long term. Similarly, the people missionaries go to reach will quickly fall away (Matt. 13:21) if their faith isn't rooted in the hope of an eternal reward. They'll be overwhelmed by the fear of death and return to the "lifelong slavery" of the devil (Heb. 2:15), just as the children of Israel wanted to. After all, "if the dead are not raised, 'Let us eat and drink, for tomorrow we die' " (1 Cor. 15:32).

A Corporate Reward

And yet in my experience, missionaries become surprisingly nervous when they speak about rewards. I understand their concern. On the field, missionaries find themselves surrounded by religious systems that offer various forms of works-based security. They worry the language of "rewards" will encourage people to try and earn God's favor or participate in a self-serving exchange where they obey God not from love but because they want to get things from him.

But this is a dangerous misconception. In healthy relationships, we do our best to reward and honor the sacrifices our loved ones make for us. We want those rewards to motivate them. C. S. Lewis reminds us:

> Indeed, if we consider the unblushing promises of reward and the staggering nature of the rewards promised in the Gospels, it would seem that Our Lord finds our desires not too strong, but too weak. . . . We must not be troubled by unbelievers when they say that this promise of reward makes the Christian life a mercenary affair. There are different kinds of rewards. There is the reward which has no natural connection with the things

> you do to earn it and is quite foreign to the desires that ought to accompany those things. Money is not the natural reward of love; that is why we call a man mercenary if he marries a woman for the sake of her money. But marriage is the proper reward for a real lover, and he is not mercenary for desiring it.[4]

In the same way, it's not self-centered for us to endure suffering in this life for the sake of a reward in the next. After all, Jesus was strengthened by his hope of a reward (Heb. 12:2). Paul was willing to suffer for the sake of others, yet he still speaks of pursuing a reward (e.g., 1 Cor. 3:14). It's crucial to understand that Jesus and Paul aren't seeking a selfish payoff or some private stash of gems they can hoard for themselves in the resurrection. Rather, the reward they want for their sufferings is an eternally glorious existence together with the God and people they love.

When my wife and I adopted our first son, some of our neighbors in the country where we serve assured us that we would receive great riches in heaven. Their words were well-meant, but something felt deeply wrong. We didn't see raising him as an ordeal that we needed to be paid back for. Far from it. It is a privilege to have our son as part of our family, and he is a greater reward than we could ever have imagined. What we want most in the next life from the love we pour into our son is for him to be there with us forever. In the same way, Paul reminds us:

> For what is our hope or joy or crown of boasting before our Lord Jesus at his coming? Is it not you? (1 Thess. 2:19)

4 C. S. Lewis, "The Weight of Glory," in *The Weight of Glory and Other Addresses* (HarperOne, 1976), 26–27. In this excellent essay, Lewis describes why love constrains us to pursue rewards, and does so with far more insight, humor, and detail than I have.

> Therefore, my brothers, whom I love and long for, my joy and crown, stand firm thus in the Lord, my beloved. (Phil. 4:1)

For Paul, both the salvation of the people he serves and the eternal life he hopes to share with them are his crown and his reward. This is exactly the type of reward that good and loving people will pursue. They can't help it. What greater reward could there be than to reign forever both with God and with the brothers and sisters he gives us (see 2 Tim. 2:12)? Paul says that we are "heirs of God and fellow heirs with Christ, provided we suffer with him in order that we may also be glorified with him (Rom. 8:17).

If it is Christ's inheritance we share, then the reward of our sufferings is incomplete without an eternal share in Christ's church as we rule the new creation together (Rev. 22:5). We will rule alongside men and women in whom the image of God been fully restored so that God's own glory, love, joy, and wisdom will be pouring out of them. They will be, as Lewis so memorably writes, creatures "which, if you saw [them] now, you would be strongly tempted to worship."[5] Their glory will be ours, and ours will be theirs. As Paul writes, "If one member is honored, all rejoice together" (1 Cor. 12:26). Missionary John Paton describes his first taste of this reward:

> At the moment when I put the bread and wine into those dark hands, once stained with the blood of cannibalism, but now stretched out to receive and partake the emblems and seals of the Redeemer's love, I had a foretaste of the joy of Glory that

5 Lewis, "The Weight of Glory," 45.

> well-nigh broke my heart to pieces. I shall never taste a deeper bliss till I gaze on the glorified face of Jesus Himself.[6]

What reward could be more fulfilling? What greater joy could await us?

A Disproportionate Reward

Scripture repeatedly concludes that our reward will be far greater than we can imagine, and that our sufferings in this life bear no comparison to it:

> For I consider that the sufferings of this present time are not worth comparing with the glory that is to be revealed to us. (Rom. 8:18)

> For this light momentary affliction is preparing for us an eternal weight of glory beyond all comparison. (2 Cor. 4:17)

Paul is not trying to diminish the difficulty of suffering or suggest that our sufferings are unimportant. Our sufferings aren't light in themselves. They're light *in comparison* with the future glory that awaits us because they're temporary and finite. But the glory we will inherit is eternal and infinite.

John makes a similar point when he compares how our sufferings give way to joy with how childbirth gives way to parenthood (John 16:21–22). No one should describe labor pains as light! But no matter how severe they are, they can't be compared to the joy of holding a newborn baby. While labor pains are short-lived, a child is a lifelong gift.

6 John Paton, *The Story of John G. Paton's Thirty Years with South Sea Cannibals*, 3rd ed. (Hodder & Stoughton, 1927), 180.

In fact, the suffering we endure to reach glory will make our promised reward more glorious. In Revelation, the elders fall before Jesus and sing:

> Worthy are you to take the scroll
>   and to open its seals,
> for you were slain, and by your blood you ransomed
>   people for God
> from every tribe and language and people and nation. (Rev. 5:9)

Do you see what's happened? Jesus's former sufferings have become part of the glory he now receives. In the same way, Jesus tells us, "Blessed are you when others revile you and persecute you and utter all kinds of evil against you falsely on my account. Rejoice and be glad, for your reward is great in heaven" (Matt. 5:11–12). It's worth repeating: our sufferings will add to the joy and glory we experience with Christ. Tim Keller writes, "Resurrection is not just consolation—it is restoration. We get it all back—the love, the loved ones, the goods, the beauties of this life—but in new, unimaginable degrees of glory and joy and strength."[7]

Our reward includes not only a glorious existence beyond death but also specific comforts for the specific sufferings we endured along the way. God will make sure that

> he who goes out weeping,
>   bearing the seed for sowing,
> shall come home with shouts of joy,
>   bringing his sheaves with him. (Ps. 126:6)

7 Timothy Keller, *Walking with God Through Pain and Suffering* (Hodder & Stoughton, 2015), 360.

While encouraging his disciples not to fear persecution, Jesus instructs them:

> I tell you, my friends, do not fear those who kill the body. . . . Are not five sparrows sold for two pennies? And not one of them is forgotten before God. Why, even the hairs of your head are all numbered. Fear not; you are of more value than many sparrows. And I tell you, everyone who acknowledges me before men, the Son of Man also will acknowledge before the angels of God. (Luke 12:4–8)

No matter how small our sufferings might be, even if they involve just a single hair falling from our heads, they will not be unacknowledged. Similarly, after describing how his disciples will be hated and persecuted (Matt. 10:34–38), Jesus insists that "the one who receives a righteous person because he is a righteous person will receive a righteous person's reward. And whoever gives one of these little ones even a cup of cold water because he is a disciple, truly, I say to you, he will by no means lose his reward" (Matt. 10:41–42). God will not forget even the smallest ways we expose ourselves to suffering by standing with Jesus and his people. Even the gift of a cup of cold water will be rewarded.

The joy we will one day inherit will only be greater for having been born out of suffering. It will not only end our sufferings or pay us back for them. It will swallow them up completely.

Conclusion

The first part of our task is finished. We've reached a foundational understanding of God's purposes for suffering in the Christian life. In chapter 2, we uncovered a story in which Satan seized control of the world through our sin, filled it with suffering and death, and uses the fear of death to hold people in slavery. In chapter 3, we saw that when Jesus gave himself as a sacrifice and rose from the dead, he set us free from Satan's slavery to the fear of death. He is leading us through this suffering-filled world to a promised land free from suffering and death. Our sufferings along the way are offered to God as a sacrifice so that others may also be set free. In this chapter, we rounded out that story, seeing that

- While we suffer in this world for the sake of others, we don't ultimately lose while they gain.
- Instead, to the extent that we share in the sufferings of Christ for the sake of others, God has a great reward waiting for us.
- Pursuing this reward is not hoping for a selfish or mercenary payoff.
- Only the hope of this reward can sustain us in our times of greatest suffering.
- The reward is to reign with Christ and share his glory with his saints for whose sake we have suffered.
- Our reward is bound up in the well-being of those for whom we love and suffer.
- Missionaries can find motivation in our service by hoping in the glory that we will share with the people we minister to.
- Our reward will be incomparably greater and infinitely longer lasting than the sufferings of this life. It will swallow up the difficulty of our sufferings altogether.

Expecting such a reward will not make our sufferings easier. Pain is pain. In the process of childbirth, the knowledge that a baby is coming doesn't make labor less painful. But it does bring hope into the process. There's a world of difference between having a baby and passing a kidney stone. Likewise, knowing the hope of our reward will keep us going on the journey to the promised land. So let us run our race with bright hope. And let's not forget God's promise: "To the one who conquers I will grant to eat of the tree of life, which is in the paradise of God" (Rev. 2:7).

5

Suffering as Ministers of the Gospel

I cared not where or how I lived, or what hardships I went through, so I could but gain souls to Christ.

DAVID BRAINERD
cited in *An Account of the Life of the Late Reverend Mr. David Brainerd*

ANYONE COULD SEE that Christie was struggling.[1] She was in the middle of her second two-year term on a remote mission field. She had a naturally buoyant personality, but something was wrong. With an apologetic smile, she explained that over the last several months, she often found herself crying for no reason. Learning the language was more difficult than she imagined, and she was still struggling with it. She had recurring bouts of stomach illness that sometimes left her immobilized for days at a time. She loved her teammates but did not always feel close to them. Being around them often left her feeling as though she didn't measure up.

1 To protect the privacy of various young missionaries my wife and I have counseled, I've rendered "Christie's" account a generic one. These are a few of the difficulties we have regularly seen in missionaries who are struggling during their first terms overseas.

Christie struggled with loneliness in ways that her teammates—even those who were single like her—seemed not to. Her singleness had been difficult before she left her home country, but she was only in her mid-twenties when she departed for the field. Now, every year that she spent single, the chance of marrying seemed less likely. She realized she was growing increasingly terrified of the possibility of lifelong singleness.

Before she left for the field, she had been part of a warm, loving church community that had helped to ease her loneliness. Now her teammates were the only friends nearby who could understand her at a deeper level, and even their well-meaning prayers left her feeling condemned. They would often pray for her to find more satisfaction in Jesus, but this left her feeling as if her depression was caused by some deeper failing in her walk with God. As hard as she prayed and as much as she struggled for joy, her despair never lifted for long. She wondered why Jesus wasn't enough for her.

Christie had grown up in a conservative Christian family. She had loved reading missionary biographies ever since she was a little girl. Even as a child, she had felt a deep excitement as she thought about following in the footsteps of Mary Slessor or Amy Carmichael. She wanted to give up everything and share Jesus's love in the world's darkest places. Christians in her circles had always encouraged her to pursue missions, and many saw her desire to serve overseas as evidence that she loved Jesus in a truly extraordinary way.

But now that she was overseas, she felt depressed and insecure. She was increasingly bitter and irritable. She had trouble concentrating on her language studies, and her mind wandered when she talked with the local people. She was hitting the wall emotionally, and it didn't seem worth it. Despite her fervent prayers, her friends and neighbors seemed entirely hard-hearted and indifferent to the gospel. Her tears flowed freely as she asked, "What's wrong with me? Why can't I be stronger? Why doesn't God help me?"

How would you respond to Christie? I trust you would speak kindly, but what would be the substance of your advice? Would you counsel her to draw closer to Jesus to find more satisfaction? To tough it out? To take a sabbatical and refocus? To leave the field?

Looking at the question more broadly, how should we as Christians respond to the difficulties of missionary life? We've spent the past three chapters describing Satan's purposes in our suffering and God's own deeper purposes as he leads us through that suffering. We've focused especially on how God works in the suffering of his people to reach lost mission fields for Christ.

Now it's time to consider some practical applications from the previous chapters. In this chapter, we begin by examining how Christians should relate to the reality of missionary suffering. Who should embrace the difficulties of missionary life? How can those who embrace these difficulties do so faithfully? This chapter is divided into three sections to address these questions and others like them.

In chapter 2, we saw that suffering is fundamentally a great evil that Satan brought into the world. Accordingly, the first section of this chapter will explore the need to avoid unnecessary suffering. In chapters 3 and 4, we saw how God calls his people to journey through certain sufferings on their way to a world beyond suffering and how this is a necessary part of the missionary task. Thus, the second section of this chapter will examine what sufferings may be "baked into" the missionary's vocation. Finally, the third section of this chapter will consider how missionaries can bear those sufferings well. In the next chapter, we broaden our focus to explore how missionaries can disciple persecuted believers and churches to respond to suffering in healthy ways.

But I want to begin with a clarification. As we saw in chapter 1, missionaries won't necessarily suffer more than other Christians.[2] After being expelled from my first country of service, I returned home from a difficult first term overseas, thinking I'd had a harder time than my friends and family.[3] Not so! Friends of mine had endured cancer, miscarriage, divorce, and bereavement. Not all my years of ministry have been as hard as that first stretch. I've spent most of my days on the mission field quite happy. Most missionaries I know would say the same.

Additionally, owing to advances in medical technology, missionaries today aren't likely to suffer in the same ways missionaries did two hundred years ago. Adoniram Judson lost his wife to disease, remarried, and endured bereavement again. John Paton buried his wife and four children in Vanuatu (formerly the New Hebrides). But while such sufferings are not common in our era, there are no guarantees in any age. I know missionaries who have lost spouses and others who have lost children. More to the point, while suffer-

2 Additionally, Christians who don't go overseas may still be called to suffer because of their ministries. For example, God may still lead Christians who don't go to the mission field to minister in unsafe neighborhoods at home. There is nothing inherently sinful about living in upscale suburbs, but it's unfortunate that it never occurs to many committed Christians to seriously consider whether God may be calling them away from a path of upward mobility if they remain at home. The resulting "flight to the suburbs" has separated many evangelical communities from suffering communities nearby that need Christ's hope. Perhaps one reason why many people in our sending countries struggle to take Christ's claims seriously is that they perceive that we have few solutions to the most painful and obvious problems around us.

3 For those unfamiliar with the rhythms of the missionary occupation, most missionaries, after spending considerable amounts of time on the field, will return home for a few weeks or months to connect with sending churches, families, and supporters. These planned returns used to be described as "furloughs." They are now commonly referred to as "home assignments" or "home ministry assignments" because of the busy schedule most missionaries have fulfilling different social or speaking engagements.

ing may not define the greater part of most missionaries' lives, the ways they handle suffering still play a vital role in their ministries as they call lost people to Christ.

Avoiding Unnecessary Suffering

Part of handling suffering well is remembering that it was Satan who brought suffering into human history and that he uses it as a powerful tool to undermine people's faith. Certainly, God has his own purposes in our suffering, but among them is his strong desire to bring us to a world that is free from suffering. Thus, suffering may be a necessary evil at times, but it is always an evil in the world and should be avoided whenever it isn't necessary.[4] God may lead us down paths of suffering on the way to the promised land, but that doesn't mean every difficult path leads in the right direction. The children of Israel learned this tragic lesson when they went to battle with the Amalekites and Canaanites despite Moses's warnings not to, and were struck down (Num. 14:40–45).

I want to strike a cautionary tone in the first section of this chapter. Discretion is the better part of valor, so we will focus first on situations in which it may be wiser and more faithful to avoid suffering. The goal here isn't to get stuck in a place of overly cautious second-guessing but to find freedom to avoid unnecessary suffering. Doing so ensures that we'll have the strength to face the sufferings that are truly necessary.

Should You Embrace the Difficulties of Missionary Life?

What sufferings does God want us to endure? Some situations are clearer than others. Sometimes, simply obeying Jesus's teachings

4 For my use of the term *evil*, see chap. 2, note 8.

leads to suffering. For example, we tell a difficult truth, and others get angry. Or we forgive those who have wronged us, giving them another opportunity to hurt us. In these types of situations, we don't need to wonder whether Jesus wants us to obey him. Of course he does!

But in more complex situations, more than one path may fall within the range of Christian obedience. Scripture doesn't mandate where you should live, whom—if anyone—you should marry, or in what capacity you should serve God and minister to others. Specifically, as we look at suffering in the missionary calling, Scripture doesn't tell you whether you should become a missionary. It also doesn't tell you what you should do if, like Christie, you are a missionary and feel overwhelmed by the difficulties you've encountered.

In these situations, the Scriptures give us a good deal of freedom to avoid suffering when we can. It's a false and pharisaical piety that assumes that the hardest path must be the holiest or that serving on a difficult mission field shows a deeper devotion to Christ than staying in one's home country. Most of us know this at some level, but we are perhaps capable of more doublethink than we imagine.

Christie, for example, may be struggling with the opinions of Christians in her circles who equate going to the field with a radical love for Christ. She may also be influenced by the opinions of her teammates who say, or at least insinuate, that her despair would go away if she could really draw near to Christ. To whatever extent Christie may be trapped under the weight of false guilt, she will be unable to move forward. She won't be able to see the choices before her as decisions that require her to wisely exercise freedom in choosing the best option. Instead, she will see them as tests that require heroism. She will believe that she is under obligation to continue on the path she has started on, no matter what it does to her.

A missionary's sending church needs to be very helpful here. Since most missionaries go to the field as young adults, they may need the help of older saints to discern how suffering will affect them over time. Commitments that seem bearable to missionary candidates in their mid twenties while surrounded by admiring church members don't always age well on lonely mission fields. We must discourage young people from thinking that the hardest decision they can make for Christ is necessarily the most God-honoring one. Similarly, we must assure them that our love and commitment remain the same, whether they stay or leave. They must not fear our judgment or disappointment if they choose another godly path.

My wife and I recently talked with a young woman who did not feel gifted to serve God overseas as a single person. Nevertheless, she was continuing toward the field with no marital prospects on the horizon at least in part because she did not feel she could tell her church the truth. She thought it would seem too unspiritual if her desire for a *man* drove her not to go to the field. It's possible that her church would have reacted more graciously than she had imagined, and she should have told the truth regardless. But her fear of man led her to hide the truth. It might also lead her into years of fruitless hardship if she embarks on a ministry she is not gifted for.

My wife and I have seen many similar situations play out, so we have some idea of how bitterly her story might end. But we were equally grieved to think that her church might be putting such pressure on her. We wish they would be more proactive in reminding her that exercising biblical caution is part of being "sold out" to Jesus. We wish they would remind her that God's kindness—not our radical acts of obedience—is the center of the gospel. God's kindness assures us that he isn't trying to grind us into the dirt. He doesn't want to wring every last ounce of painful obedience from us.

He's not interested in testing the outer limits of how much we will sacrifice for him as we slowly collapse. Instead, he wants us to trust his kindness by embracing the freedom he has given us to make wise decisions about which life paths to choose.

Encountering Suffering Soberly

What does it look like to make such wise decisions? Almost immediately after Paul calls us to offer our bodies as a "living sacrifice" to God, he says:

> For by the grace given to me I say to everyone among you not to think of himself more highly than he ought to think, but to think with sober judgment, each according to the measure of faith that God has assigned. For as in one body we have many members, and the members do not all have the same function, so we, though many, are one body in Christ, and individually members one of another. Having gifts that differ according to the grace given to us, let us use them: if prophecy, in proportion to our faith; if service, in our serving; the one who teaches, in his teaching; the one who exhorts, in his exhortation; the one who contributes, in generosity; the one who leads, with zeal; the one who does acts of mercy, with cheerfulness. (Rom. 12:3–8)

While we must offer ourselves as living sacrifices to God, we also shouldn't think too highly of our readiness to do so. We are weak, so we should offer ourselves as living sacrifices to God only in the ways God gives us strength for. There are gifts God hasn't enabled us to give, ministries he hasn't called us to lead, and acts of mercy he hasn't equipped us to participate in. In each of these examples, we are limited in our service to Christ not because we don't think he is worthy of more but because he has not given us the ability—in Paul's words, the "grace"—to joyfully give of ourselves beyond a certain point.

So as we face decisions about life or ministry, we need "sober judgment" (Rom. 12:3) to help us discern how we can glorify God according to "the grace given to us" (Rom. 12:6).[5] Part of this discernment involves examining the "generosity" and "cheerfulness" that God gives us to participate in different ministries. For example, the earnest willingness of the Macedonians' giving (2 Cor. 8:4) is evidence of "the grace of God that has been given" (2 Cor. 8:1) to them to give above and beyond their ability. Paul doesn't want people to give if God hasn't put a willing cheerfulness in their hearts (2 Cor. 9:7). Similarly, the ability of some singles to remain relatively undistracted by their desires for companionship and intimacy is a sign that God may have gifted them with singleness (1 Cor. 7:7–9). Otherwise, Paul instructs them to pursue marriage.

This doesn't mean that we simply choose whatever ministry we think will maximize our earthly happiness. Instead, the grace and cheerfulness Paul describes includes a special strength God gives us to look past the earthly difficulties entailed in some ministries—and not others—to the reward that awaits. For example, when Paul says, "I will most gladly spend and be spent for your souls" (2 Cor. 12:15), he is expressing a desire for the Corinthians' eternal well-being that prepares him to endure great earthly suffering for their sake. This desire and the cheerfulness it brings even amid suffering are indicators that God has given Paul "grace" for his ministry to

5 It's not my intention here to fully detail how we should determine our giftedness for missionary work. Instead, in this chapter, I intend to examine how our ability to bear the hardships of ministry life may affect that decision. For those who are interested in a fuller description of how we can assess our giftedness for the field, see Matt Rhodes, *No Shortcut to Success: A Manifesto for Modern Missions* (Crossway, 2022), 204–23.

Corinth. As the Scriptures shape our hearts, the Holy Spirit renews our desires in the same way, enabling us to cheerfully look past any earthly sufferings we face while we pursue the ministries he has given us grace to do. That means people who are gifted to serve God as missionaries will generally be able to maintain the joy and desire to complete their task as they focus on their eternal reward, despite any difficulties, sufferings, and sadnesses.

For example, shortly before leaving for Burma, Ann Judson wrote to her friend Lydia Kimball:

> I have about come to the determination to give up all my comforts and enjoyments here, sacrifice my affection to relatives and friends, and go where God in his providence, shall see fit to place me. My determinations are not hasty, or formed without viewing the dangers, trials, and hardships attendant on a missionary life.[6]

This wasn't a flippant decision. Ann Judson exercised sober judgment and found the cheerfulness Paul speaks of to go to the field—not a bubbly, emotional froth but a settled conviction, despite the dangers and trials that await. That's why she could say, "Might I but be the means of converting a single soul, it would be worth spending all my days to accomplish."[7] Her clear-sighted conviction was rooted not in the hope of thriving overseas but in the desire of an eternal reward. She knew that "all [her] days" on earth would pass in the blink of an eye, but the souls she went to reach who believed the gospel would join her in glory through endless ages.

6 Ann Judson, in Vance Christie, *Adoniram Judson: Devoted for Life* (Christian Focus, 2013), chap. 4, Kindle.

7 Ann Judson, in Christie, *Adoniram Judson*, chap. 4, Kindle.

Here's the problem: In this life, "we see in a mirror dimly" (1 Cor. 13:12). For some ministries, God does not give us the grace to look past our sufferings, but we may not quite realize it and thus may continue to press forward. Ministries and life situations we are not given this grace for will tax us in overwhelming ways. As a result, they can distract us from God or even tempt us and lead us into sin (see, e.g., 1 Cor. 7:2, 32–34).

I have a genuine pastoral concern for missionaries because they often have a natural intensity that can lead them to embrace sufferings that they are ill-equipped to handle. This intensity is part of what helps them make it to the field, but it is not a spiritual quality. Unless it is governed with real spiritual maturity, it can enable them not only to endure suffering for Christ's sake but also to exhibit a harsh and demanding nature toward themselves, their families, and their teammates.

In my years on the mission field, I have seen many well-meaning missionaries exceed their limits, sometimes to the point of personal collapse. I have watched singles ill-suited to singleness quietly consume themselves with loneliness as they watched the solitary years slip by on the remotest of mission fields. All the while, they wondered if their discontent somehow meant they needed to press harder into Jesus. I've seen families that were already struggling to function insist on pushing toward more rugged and distant fields. I've watched couples sink under the stress of raising children in another culture and have seen them blame each other because one was weak while the other was strong.

If you find yourself struggling with suffering that you don't have the grace to bear, my prayer is that you will find freedom to choose other paths. Perhaps find a mission field you are better suited for, take time off the field to recover, or even find a different vocation back in your country of origin. God has chosen to work through our weaknesses as well as our strengths. We don't glorify him by making choices that refuse to acknowledge the specific weaknesses he's left us with.

Avoiding Unnecessary Suffering on the Mission Field

It's important to avoid unnecessary suffering not only when deciding if we belong in overseas ministry but also once we arrive on the field. This may seem counterintuitive since I've spent two chapters arguing that God uses suffering to redeem the world. That's true, but sin, war, and cancer also play a role in God's plan to redeem the world, and yet God expects us to avoid them if possible. The fact that God has greater purposes for the evils he allows doesn't negate the fact that they are evil. We are not called to seek suffering itself but the redemption of suffering.

Nevertheless, it's possible—especially, perhaps, for missionaries with intense personalities—to become so fascinated by the horrors that God's people endure for his sake that we begin to see suffering and martyrdom as desirable outcomes, as some Christians did during Rome's fiercest purges.[8] Christian author Alan Noble warns of an unfortunate tendency for some evangelicals to "fetishize suffering" by seeing it as inherently virtuous.[9] Sadly, you don't have to look far in missionary literature to find examples of this today.

Thankfully, the wider church has historically avoided this pitfall.[10] Even during the most horrific persecutions, those who

8 For example, the early theologian Tertullian argued that Christ's instruction to flee persecution was only temporary. See Tertullian, *De fugu in persecutione* 4, 6.

9 Alan Noble, "The Evangelical Persecution Complex: The Theological and Cultural Roots of a Damaging Attitude in the Christian Community," *Atlantic*, August 4, 2014, https://www.theatlantic.com/.

10 Early Christian writings, such as *The Martyrdom of Polycarp*, criticize those who "come forward [to be martyred] of their own accord, since the gospel does not teach us to do so,"

"rushed on death" were widely seen as "false martyrs" whom "Christ would desert."[11] Thus, when the early martyrs Polycarp and Cyprian of Carthage were captured, they were brave enough to die and did not deny their faith, but they still hid from capture while they could. Their example of withdrawing from persecution is mirrored at various points by Athanasius, Martin Luther, John Calvin, William Tyndale, Corrie ten Boom, Dietrich Bonhoeffer, Peter, Paul, and Christ himself.[12] It is after many years of withdrawing from their enemies that Christ and Paul finally go where they know they will be captured. Christ did so because the time had come for him to die for the world (John 17:1), and Paul did because he was "constrained by the Spirit" to do so (Acts 20:22). God may call us to confront such dangers, but we should exercise real caution in claiming equivalence between our own callings and theirs.

After all, Jesus himself says, "When they persecute you in one town, flee to the next" (Matt. 10:23). There's nothing cowardly or selfish about this. It isn't giving in to the enemy. It's living to fight the enemy another day. Jesus knows as he instructs his apostles to flee persecution that a time will come for most of them to give their lives in martyrdom. But none of them walk into

---

and even recount the story of Quintus, who, in his fleshly thinking, offered himself up for martyrdom, then recanted upon seeing the beasts. See "The Martyrdom of Saint Polycarp," in *Early Christian Fathers*, ed. Cyril C. Richardson (Simon and Schuster, 1995), 150.

11 For examples of those who "rushed on death," see Clement of Alexandria, *The Stromata, or Miscellanies*, trans. by William Wilson, in *Ante-Nicene Fathers: Translations of the Writings of the Fathers Down to A.D. 325*, ed. Alexander Roberts, James Donaldson, and A. Cleveland Coxe (Buffalo, NY: 1885), 2:411–12. See also Justo L. Gonzalez, *The Story of Christianity*, vol 1, *The Early Church to the Reformation* (HarperOne, 2010), 55.

12 Peter flees when Herod wants to kill him (Acts 12:17). Paul flees persecution at multiple points in the book of Acts (e.g., Acts 9:25; 13:50; 14:5–6; 17:5–10, 14; 20:1). Jesus flees persecution at many points in the Gospels (e.g., Matt. 12:14–15; Luke 4:29–30; John 8:59; 10:39).

martyrdom intentionally.[13] Even the second-century theologian Origen, whose mother reportedly hid his clothes to prevent him from volunteering as a martyr when he was a young man, later admitted, "It is not dishonorable to avoid exposing oneself to dangers . . . when this is done, not through fear of death, but from a desire to benefit others by remaining in life until the proper time."[14]

It concerns me when I find young missionary candidates disproportionately drawn to countries with the highest risk of persecution. I'm not suggesting that we should give up on these countries because of persecution, but all other things being equal, the presence of high-level persecution should not draw us to an area to plant churches. Even the worst persecutions in history have come and gone, and our work may be more successful if we take advantage of the lulls in persecution that occur. In Acts 8, when persecution results in the murder of Stephen and others (Acts 7:60; 8:3; 26:10), many of the disciples leave Jerusalem and minister in places where such persecution is less likely. Their ability to minister freely elsewhere results in great fruit (cf. 1 Tim. 2:2–4).[15] But if we default to imagining that the most faithful response is always to head toward suffering, we may short-circuit our own ability to minister. My own ministry in my first country

13 Some may argue that Paul goes to Jerusalem knowing he will be imprisoned. While this is true, throughout his imprisonment Paul attempts to secure his release (e.g., Acts 23:6, 16–17; 24:10–21; 25:10–11; 2 Tim 4:16). Martyrdom is never his intent (Phil. 1:25–26), though he is willing to die for Christ when the time comes.

14 Origen, *Contra Celsum*, quoted in Ruth Sutcliffe, "To Flee or Not to Flee? Matthew 10:23 and Third Century Flight in Persecution," *Scrinium* 14 (2018): 149. The account of his mother hiding his clothes can be found in *The Church History of Eusebius*, trans. Arthur Cushman McGiffert (Eerdmans, 2019), 258.

15 In 1 Timothy 2:2–4, Paul seems to assume that, generally, it is when the church is at peace and not when it is persecuted that we find ideal situations for "people to be saved."

of service ended before any real fruit became evident when I was expelled by an Islamist government. If we prioritize sending missionaries to the unreached areas where people are most hostile to the gospel simply because of their hostility, we may see many missionaries' ministries cut short prematurely and before they can bear fruit.

Additionally, we shouldn't overestimate our strength by walking into suffering unnecessarily. On the night of his betrayal, Jesus tells his disciples to pray that they may "not enter into temptation" (Matt. 26:41). In the Lord's Prayer, he teaches us to pray something similar:

> And lead us not into temptation,
> but deliver us from evil. (Matt. 6:13)

In both cases, the Greek word rendered "temptation" (*peirasmon*) can equally be translated as "trial" (e.g., Acts 20:19; James 1:2). Jesus is warning us to pray not only that we may be spared from being enticed to do evil but also that we may be spared from evil times. He is practical enough to know that all hardships bring temptations. So "deliver us from evil" consciously echoes similar requests in the Old Testament to avoid persecution:

> Deliver me, O Lord, from evil men;
> preserve me from violent men. (Ps. 140:1;
> cf. 59:2; 97:10)

If we pray that God will spare us from evil times, we should also do what we can to avoid them. We are all weaker than we imagine.

> The prudent sees danger and hides himself,
> but the simple go on and suffer for it. (Prov. 22:3)

What Should Missionaries Be Ready to Suffer?

Now I'd like to change focus. The Scriptures teach us to avoid unhealthy suffering, but they don't give us room to avoid suffering altogether. Their caution isn't meant to paralyze us but to help us make good decisions so that we'll have confidence as we face whatever sufferings wisdom calls us to endure. We have noted that not everyone is gifted for missionary service. But many people are given the grace to serve Christ as missionaries. What difficulties must they prepare themselves to cheerfully bear as they look to an eternal reward?

As we saw in chapter 3, a good deal of the difficulty we face is simply the price tag of being among the people we hope to minister to. Just as Peter said to Jesus, "See, we have left everything and followed you" (Matt. 19:27), so missionaries today must also leave their homes and families behind to serve, immersing themselves in an unfamiliar way of life among a people who may initially be quite hostile to them and their message. In some cases, the family members they leave behind may not understand the choice to go and may respond with painful accusations or rejection. Far from their loved ones and sometimes enduring difficult living conditions, they may find themselves "unknown," "sorrowful," "poor," and "having nothing" (2 Cor. 6:9–10).

It usually takes years of difficult, full-time study to master the language and culture. During these years, disorientation and cultural frustration set in. We can't understand what people are saying and are often the object of their jokes. Their foods are strange and distasteful. The ways they relate to us may seem either cold and aloof or overly friendly and invasive of our privacy. We watch our loved ones struggle to accept a new way of life. Our message may be widely rejected. Corrupt government officials may pressure us for money. Perhaps none of these difficulties on their own would faze us, but together they can wear us out. And in addition to the slow grind of small losses, there will be moments of acute difficulty. There may be incapacitating bouts of sickness for those who work in poverty-stricken areas. At times, we may endure harassment, threats, or even violent attacks from people who oppose our message.

But we need not be discouraged. God not only gives us grace to bear all these difficulties, but is also at work in them. Our sufferings are not just the price that allows us to be among the people we are ministering to. They also demonstrate the truth of the gospel to people around us. Remember, our suffering is a spectacle—a theater—for them to see the gospel enacted (1 Cor. 4:9).

In unreached areas, the demonstration of God's redemptive power amid our sufferings may be more necessary than we imagine. Some years ago, a missionary told me about a time when he shared a Bible verse with a Muslim friend, who responded, "Now I know that Christianity is true." The missionary was shocked, so he asked his friend if he wanted to become a Christian. To his surprise, his friend was equally shocked. He did not yet know it was possible for him to become a Christian.

People know that it is possible for you or me to follow Jesus, but they may not realize that it possible for them, in their particular circumstances and lives, to follow Jesus. My friend Arbab put it this way: "I became a Christian a few months ago. I had wanted to become a Christian for many years, ever since I was a child. But I didn't know how to. There were no Christians where we lived. The government does very bad things to people who leave Islam, and their families do too. So I didn't think I could." For years, Arbab didn't imagine it was possible to bear the pressure and suffering his community would inflict on him if he followed Christ. He didn't know how to live out the Christian life in such a difficult situation. Ultimately, he needed missionaries not only to tell him about Christ but also to take time to show him how to live a joyful Christian life in his own context—to act out their message within his cultural constraints, facing similar sufferings and circumstances to those he faces.

Seeing God sustain us despite separation from our families and homelands may help new believers bear the threat of being expelled from their own families and communities. Seeing God sustain us in any physical pain or persecution may give new believers strength to confess Christ when they fear violence from their communities. If God ordains it, then we must be ready to remain faithful amid suffering and persecution alongside new believers. Christian history is filled with stories of missionaries who were not only rejected and insulted but also imprisoned, tortured, martyred, and bereaved, and the proclamation of Christ can still lead to any of these outcomes today. We may not encounter the same hardships the New Testament missionaries did, but we cannot afford to be unprepared if we should have to bear them.

In fact, Paul sees his suffering and Timothy's as a direct result of their missionary calling. He says to Timothy:

> I was appointed a preacher and apostle and teacher, which is why I suffer as I do. (2 Tim. 1:11–12)

> As for you, always be sober-minded, endure suffering, do the work of an evangelist, fulfill your ministry. (2 Tim. 4:5)

As Paul and Timothy bore witness to the truth—Paul by teaching and Timothy by doing "the work of an evangelist"—the lies that Satan used to hold people captive were exposed.[16] That's why Revelation tells us that the victorious saints "have conquered him by the blood of the Lamb *and by the word of their testimony*" (Rev. 12:11). Missionaries who teach God's word clearly pose a direct threat to the systems through which Satan rules the world. It's not surprising that he responds to their ministries with persecution. I've argued elsewhere that communicating God's message is the missionary's central task, so we need to be prepared for persecution.[17] If we're doing our job well—and if God is breathing on his word to open the eyes of the lost—then persecution is a real possibility. Again, endurance is crucial. Some people may only find the courage to face persecution after we demonstrate what it looks like to follow Christ through suffering over the long term.

That's one reason why I remain deeply concerned when proponents of modern "movements methods" suggest that it's normal for churches to grow so rapidly that brand-new churches plant other new churches after a few months. For example, recent research among missionaries who have reported success using a "disciple-making movements" (DMM) approach among unreached peoples claims that, on average, only forty-two months elapsed between the missionaries' arrival and the targeted "DMM threshold," defined as "more than a hundred churches planted, four or more generations

16 This is a clear pattern in the New Testament. Paul teaches, and when his enemies are powerless to refute him, they riot (e.g., Acts 17:5), have him imprisoned (Acts 16:23), beat him (Acts 21:27–33), or stone him (Acts 14:19). Stephen's enemies can't refute his teaching (Acts 6:10), so they murder him (Acts 7:58–60). Jesus's enemies can't refute his teaching in the temple (Matt. 22–25), so they crucify him.

17 Rhodes, *No Shortcut to Success*, 111–22.

deep."[18] Some missionaries reported reaching this stage after only three months.[19] That means that, on average, even if missionaries had begun planting churches among these unreached groups the moment they arrived—often without knowing their languages—new churches would have had to form and reproduce every ten months. A new church would have been planted, on average, every thirteen days. In the faster scenarios, it would have taken only three weeks for new churches to grow and reproduce, and on average, a new church would have been planted every single day.

I've described my concerns with movements methods elsewhere, so I'll restrict my comments to examining these methods in light of what we've seen regarding suffering and the missionary task.[20] I'm concerned that the widespread promotion of shortened time frames doesn't set up young missionaries for success. Missionaries who are sent out expecting immediate, explosive church growth will have difficulty shifting their mindset to endure long years or decades overseas.

Moreover, the explosive growth of new churches reported by practitioners of such methods doesn't correspond with what the Scriptures show us about church growth in persecuted areas. For example, leading movements-methods proponents Warrick Farah and Alan Hirsch write, "God has quietly brought 1% of the world into his Kingdom through church planting movements in the past 25 years, mostly among Hindus and Muslims."[21] They get this

18 Samuel Kebreab, "Observations over Fifteen Years of Disciple Making Movements," in *Motus Dei: The Movement of God to Disciple the Nations*, ed. W. Farah (William Carey, 2021), 31.

19 Kebreab, "Observations over Fifteen Years," 32.

20 See Rhodes, *No Shortcut to Success*, 47–107; Rhodes, "Advancing Conversations About Proclamational and Movements Methodologies," *Global Missiology* 19, no. 3 (2022): 18–29.

21 Warrick Farah and Alan Hirsch, "Movemental Ecclesiology: Recalibrating Church for the Next Frontier," Arab Baptist Theological Seminary, April 15, 2021, https://www.abtslebanon.org.

number from the research of Justin Long, who has since written that the number has now ballooned to 114 million people.[22] Of course, we should never rejoice in the persecution of our brothers and sisters, but in chapter 2 we saw how persecution functions in the unreached world, so the claim that over 100 million people—mostly Hindus and Muslims—have been added "quietly" to God's kingdom should give us pause.

Muslim-background believer Anwar Hossein describes how the size of a movement in his own country was exaggerated: "If it had been true then definitely there would be newspaper reports everywhere, television and charges, but nobody knows. Because [embracing new religious ideas] is a very hot issue."[23] A massive and growing demographic shift like the one Farah, Hirsch, and Long describe would not only pique the attention of reporters but also lead to widespread persecution, including martyrdom and large numbers of new believers being exiled from their communities.[24] If such events are happening, how are they hidden from public view? Why are they reported anecdotally and only within the missions community? Could it be that the people reporting such numbers have unintentionally misrepresented what is actually happening?

22 Justin Long, "How Long to Reach the Goal?," *Mission Frontiers* 45, no. 1 (2023): 34.

23 Anwar Hossein, interview by Bill Nikides in Joshua B. Lingel and Bill Nikides, *Chrislam: How Missionaries Are Promoting an Islamized Gospel* (i2 Ministries, 2011), chap. 5, Kindle.

24 Indeed, the slower, steady growth of the church over generations in Nepal from no Christians in 1951 to approximately half a million in the early 2020s has sparked widespread international interest, including reporting from secular news sources. For example, see Kevin Kim and Rebecca Henshcke, "Christian Missionaries Target the Birthplace of Buddha in Nepal," BBC, January 14, 2023, https://www.bbc.com. Additionally, while some Nepalese Christians have suggested that these numbers are intentionally underestimated, they are supported by census figures confirming the growth of churches. Such expansion on the scale observed in Nepal is difficult to hide. Surely, then, growth of the type claimed by movements proponents in South Asia would have some sort of external confirmation, whether in census figures, news reports, or elsewhere.

After all, their reports are often plagued by dubious statistical methods.[25] Furthermore, observations from the field increasingly find that the massive numbers in many of these reports may be exaggerated or altogether hollow.

Even if we imagine that the church growth numbers are correct, movements that grow so rapidly will likely be immature in many ways. It might be possible to share bare outlines of the gospel's plan for justification from sin in ways that people can understand in such a short time. But it's not possible to raise up mature leaders for these rapidly burgeoning churches who will be able to offer patient instruction on how to walk with Christ.

Moreover, how will these churches respond when suffering comes? Certainly, there isn't time for them to observe God's resurrection power in the theater of our suffering among them. The author of Hebrews tells his suffering readers, "Remember . . . those who spoke to you the word of God. Consider the outcome of their way of life, and imitate their faith" (Heb. 13:7). When a few weeks or months elapse before each new church is planted, how will new believers have time to know the outcome of our faith and way of life? If they have no opportunity to observe God's faithfulness in our sufferings, they will be missing a key source of encouragement to endure the sufferings they encounter in their own lives.

Proponents of these newer methods are brothers and sisters in Christ. I'm not calling anyone's sincerity into question, and I'm confident that any exaggerated reports are unintentional. Nevertheless, reports of rapid success often encourage earnest young missionaries to work more quickly than they should, which causes

25 See Rhodes, *No Shortcut to Success*, 47–66; Rhodes, "Advancing Conversations."

real damage to real people and hurts the cause of the gospel. It can lead missionaries to leave churches behind in which the people don't know the word and who are unprepared for suffering.

We ought to tone down the focus on speed. Slow progress doesn't mean that we're on the wrong path. Of course, working slowly is not the ultimate goal. Like speed, it can be overemphasized. But in our day, when church growth and missions strategists are fascinated with speed and reproducibility, I suspect this reminder may be timely.

Bearing Suffering Well

How do we find courage for long seasons of suffering or for the dry periods of ministry when our prayers seem to remain unanswered for years? If it's true that suffering is both a normal part of the Christian life and a great evil in the world, then we shouldn't expect to attain a level of spiritual transcendence in which we no longer feel shaken or discouraged. However courageous we may feel at our best moments, we will feel alone and forsaken in our times of greatest suffering. All Christians feel this way, and if we don't, we probably just aren't suffering very much yet. John Calvin writes, "The saints could show no patience under the cross if they were not both tortured with pain and grievously molested. Were there no hardship in poverty, no pain in disease, no sting in ignominy, no fear in death, where would be the fortitude and moderation in enduring them?"[26]

Despite their courageous convictions, history's great missionaries struggled with weakness as we would. Adoniram Judson "suffered much from a peculiar form of dread of death," to the extent that

26 John Calvin, *Institutes of the Christian Religion*, trans. Henry Beveridge (Calvin Translation Society, 1845), 280.

he had a grave dug so that he could stare into it in meditation.[27] David Brainerd wrestled with a sense of his own sinfulness and lack of compassion as he prayed for the lost.[28] His good friend Jonathan Edwards noted his dark struggles with the "disease of melancholy" and his "disposition to dejection."[29] At one point, Brainerd wrote, "I was in a great degree of despair about ever doing or seeing any good 'in the land of the living.' . . . [I] was so overwhelmed with dejection that I knew not how to live. I longed for death exceedingly; my soul was sunk into deep waters and the floods were ready to drown me."[30] And Jim Elliot complained, "Satan and the flesh have been on me hard. How God holds my soul in His life and permits one with such wretchedness to continue in his service I cannot tell."[31]

These missionaries aren't alone—the saints of Scripture felt the same way. Job questioned God's goodness (Job 3:1–26). Paul tells the Corinthians he "despaired of life itself" (2 Cor. 1:8). When Jesus tells his disciples, "My soul is very sorrowful," in the garden of Gethsemane (Matt. 26:38), he's quoting Psalm 42:5.[32] We shouldn't forget what a dark emotional place Jesus was identifying with when he quoted such a despairing psalm. The psalmist writes,

27 Francis Wayland, *A Memoir of the Life and Labors of the Rev. Adoniram Judson, D.D.* (Phillips, Sampson, 1853), 1:536.

28 Jonathan Edwards, *An Account of the Life of the Late Reverend Mr. David Brainerd* (Applewood Books, 1749), 46, 220.

29 Edwards, *Brainerd*, vi, ix.

30 Edwards, *Brainerd*, 137.

31 *The Journals of Jim Elliot: Martyr, Missionary, Man of God*, ed. Elisabeth Elliot (Revell, 1978), 475.

32 The Greek words Jesus uses for "soul" (*psychē*) and for "sorrowful" (*perilypos*) are the exact same words used in Ps. 42:5 for "soul" and "cast down" in the Septuagint, the Greek translation of the Old Testament that was available in Jesus's day. These two words are not used together anywhere else in Scripture.

> My tears have been my food
> day and night. (Ps. 42:3)

He's too distressed and hopeless to eat, and he lies awake late at night weeping.

For those who struggle with despair, I want to emphasize a significant point. The Scriptures never imply that very dark moments—or even longer seasons of depression—indicate any kind of failure in your spiritual life. C. S. Lewis says that "some of [God's] special favorites have gone through longer and deeper troughs than anyone else."[33] The Scriptures refuse to suggest that if we were stronger spiritually, then we wouldn't be prone to such lows. They refuse to deny or overlook the terrible difficulty of the circumstances we sometimes go through. They never tell us to rise above our difficulties, transcend our circumstances, or pull ourselves up by our bootstraps. Far too often, however, that's what we imagine we should do. I've heard many Christians tell each other that real, godly joy is independent of circumstances. But the Scriptures tell us something different: They tell us that our circumstances are too much for us to master and that suffering can crush us. Christ himself didn't rise above difficult circumstances. He didn't whistle in the dark on his way to Calvary. Instead, he groaned in his sufferings, cried out amid his sufferings, and finally died of his sufferings.

The Scriptures fully acknowledge the darkness of human suffering, but they also teach us to have hope because God is at work in our circumstances. They tell us that, yes, the world is all wrong now and things aren't at all as they should be. And yes, we certainly lack the strength to endure it as we should. But all that

33 C. S. Lewis, *The Screwtape Letters* (Zondervan, 2001), 38.

is the smaller part of the truth. As we saw in chapter 4, the greater part of the truth is that God will reward us in real ways and redeem all our difficulties. God is not unmoved by our sufferings. He still knows every hair on our heads (Luke 12:7) and keeps all our tears in his bottle (Ps. 56:8). He will even resurrect the dead (1 Cor. 15:20, 42–49) and set right everything that is wrong on the earth (Rev. 21:4–7).

As missionaries, we must remember these truths in our lowest moments. If we offer these moments to God as a sacrifice, then a glorious reward is waiting. God has promised that some from every tribe and language and people and nation (Rev. 7:9) will worship Jesus in eternity. One day, whether we see it in this lifetime or not, our prayers for the people we minister to will be answered. He will bring some of them to himself, and we will worship him and reign over the new creation together with them in indescribable joy and glory (Rev. 20:4–5). Our sufferings and service to God will be rewarded. This is the knowledge that sustains us through suffering.

Complaining to God

Thus, we need to respond to suffering by crying out to God for the reward and redemption he has promised. Our prayers play an important role in bringing that deliverance, and they should express both our desire for deliverance and the difficulty we're enduring. In Psalm 42, the psalmist not only asks for help but also complains to God in his misery. He writes:

> I say to God, my rock:
>   "Why have you forgotten me?
> Why do I go mourning
>   because of the oppression of the enemy?" (Ps. 42:9)

We need to be careful here. There's a world of difference between complaining *to* God and grumbling *against* God. The children of Israel grumble against God in the desert when they say, "Would that we had died by the hand of the LORD in the land of Egypt . . . for you have brought us out into this wilderness to kill this whole assembly with hunger" (Ex. 16:3). The Israelites aren't coming to God asking for answers or deliverance. They're not asking questions. Instead, they're passing judgment on God because the path they're on isn't the path they want. Despite his consistent, miraculous provision, the Israelites are forsaking him.

In Psalm 42, the psalmist approaches God differently. Overwhelmed by his pain, he complains and expresses his confusion about why God hasn't helped him. But rather than concluding, as the children of Israel did in the desert, that God can't be trusted, the psalmist turns to God for deliverance. Even in his despair, he does not give up hope that God will rescue him.

Look again at his complaint: "Why have you forgotten me?" In the Old Testament, for God to "remember" someone was to decide to act on that person's behalf.[34] So the psalmist is pleading with God to act on his behalf. We will experience similar confusion, and in our darkest seasons, we'll need to pour out our struggles to God in prayer. We must plead with him to act, reach into our difficulties, and deliver us.

Speaking Truth to Our Souls

But how do we cling to God's promises as we wait for his deliverance? Any biblical exploration of the role of suffering in the

34 For example, just before God frees Israel from slavery he says to Moses, "I have heard the groaning of the people of Israel whom the Egyptians hold as slaves, and I have *remembered* my covenant" (Ex. 6:5). By saying that he remembers his covenant, God means that he is about to act.

Christian life will uncover this lesson: The pattern, not the exception, in the Bible is people enduring for a long time as they wait for God's redemption. Abraham waited eighteen years for God to fulfill his promise of a son (Gen. 21:1–7). Joseph spent years enslaved and in prison before his dreams of his brothers bowing down to him came to fruition (Gen. 37:1–11; 40–41). David spent years running from Saul after he received God's anointing (1 Sam. 23:15–24:22; 26:1–25). Most missionaries will wait too. God takes us on long journeys, and he will get us to our destination. But he rarely does so quickly or without our suffering along the way.

So how do we strengthen ourselves to stay faithful as we face the long, difficult seasons of waiting? The psalmist wrestles with his despair by reminding himself to maintain hope as he waits for God to redeem his troubles. He says:

> Why are you cast down, O my soul,
>   and why are you in turmoil within me?
> Hope in God; for I shall again praise him,
>   my salvation and my God. (Ps. 42:5–6; cf. 42:11)

In our most troubled seasons, we often hear our soul muttering despairing narratives. I have certainly heard them in my darker hours: "You should never have become a missionary. These people are too hard-hearted. You're too spiritually weak. You aren't gifted enough. You still struggle too much with sin and hypocrisy. You must have taken a wrong turn somewhere in life. God isn't in your work."

A similar thing seems to have happened to the psalmist. His soul is cast down, and it is depressing him. Everything he sees is terrible. So in Psalm 42:5 and 11, we see the psalmist fighting to reorient his soul to the Lord. In his classic book *Spiritual Depression*, D. Martyn Lloyd-Jones describes the psalmist's response:

> The main art in spiritual living is to know how to handle yourself. You have to take yourself in hand, you have to address yourself, preach to yourself, question yourself. You must say to your soul, "Why are you cast down?" What business do you have to be disquieted? You must turn on yourself instead of muttering in this depressed, unhappy way . . . and say to yourself, "Hope thou in God."[35]

Do you see what Lloyd-Jones is saying? We don't have the wisdom or strength to handle these hard times. We need a wisdom and a righteousness from above that we can preach to ourselves to set us on the correct path. We need to turn to the Scriptures and lean on God's strong promises. We need to wrestle with our souls and remind them of the truth.

None of these patterns—either the confusion in our suffering or the need to preach to ourselves—indicates a substandard Christian life. Rather, it's the ordinary path for how God's people handle their difficulties. Like the psalmist, we need to remind ourselves of God's goodness and the hope that awaits us. When we face difficulties in our ministry, we need to remind ourselves that one day every nation will be won for Christ, and God will make our suffering worthwhile.

We'll also need to reach out to our brothers and sisters. Dietrich Bonhoeffer writes:

> God has willed that we should seek and find God's living Word in the testimony of other Christians, in the mouths of human

35 D. Martin Lloyd Jones, *Spiritual Depression: Its Causes and Cure* (Zondervan, 2016), 21.

> beings. Therefore, Christians need other Christians who speak God's Word to them. . . . The Christ in their own hearts is weaker than the Christ in the word of other Christians. Their own hearts are uncertain, those of their brothers and sisters are sure.[36]

There are times we need to borrow faith from a friend. Missionaries will need to lean heavily on teammates or friends and family back home. Again, this isn't an indication that we're living a substandard Christian life. Far from it! God has designed the Christian life so that we are dependent on each other. We are limited in our ability to discover God's goodness on our own. We're not meant to live the Christian life alone. The author of Hebrews reminds his suffering readers multiple times to encourage each other and take courage from the example of others whom God has rewarded (Heb. 3:13; 4:1; 10:24–25; 11:1–12:4; 13:7).We're meant to be spurred on by a great cloud of witnesses, those who have gone before us and those who walk beside us.

Ultimately, there may be moments when despair takes hold of us, despite all our efforts to hold on to hope. You've reminded yourself of the promises of Scripture, wrestled with your soul, and reached out to friends. But despair still engulfs you. This has happened to me. But even when we can't feel hope, there is still hope. David writes:

> I had said in my alarm,
> "I am cut off from your sight."
> But you heard the voice of my pleas for mercy
> when I cried to you for help. (Ps. 31:22)

36 Dietrich Bonhoeffer, "Life Together," in *Dietrich Bonhoeffer Works*, vol. 5, trans. Daniel W. Bloesch, ed. Gerhard Ludwig Müller and Albrecht Schönherr (Fortress, 1996), chap. 1, Kindle.

It was God's faithfulness to rescue David—not David's ability to feel hopeful—that ultimately sustained David. God will rescue you, too, whether you feel like he will or not. Knowing this doesn't make pain less painful or fear less fearful or despair less dark. But it keeps us holding on until God himself brings redemption.

Conclusion

Let's return to Christie's story. What wisdom might we offer her as she struggles with despair? To begin, Christie should focus on stabilizing herself as much as possible before making any long-term decisions. This will involve both reaching out to others for advice and support and finding whatever emotional equilibrium she can. She may need to remove herself temporarily from whatever parts of the problem are hardest for her to deal with. Once she finds a stable place where she can make decisions about her future, Christie should explore whether God has given her the "grace" to serve him joyfully in her current situation. If he has not, she may need to return home or to search for another field situation for which she does have the grace—perhaps serving on a less remote field, as a married woman if the opportunity arises, or on a different team. We should remind Christie that she will not be a second-class Christian who isn't fully committed if she chooses to leave her current post.

But perhaps Christie is simply going through a long low period in her life, or perhaps she is experiencing a slow, painful adjustment in her expectations. After the low period passes or she recalibrates her expectations, she may discover that God has given her the grace to stay. Her life may still have many more low points, but even in her low points she will increasingly find the ability to "most gladly spend and be spent" (2 Cor. 12:15) for those she is working among. As she anticipates years in the field—facing whatever sickness, loneliness, living conditions, or even persecution she may encounter—her confidence will grow; knowing the privilege of serving among these people makes it all worth it.

Looking beyond Christie's story, here are some takeaways for missionaries and missionary candidates more generally:

- Suffering reveals the brokenness and evil of this world, and we should avoid it when possible.
- Missionaries won't necessarily suffer more than other believers, but their work may involve facing unusual difficulties if they want to minister effectively.
- In deciding whether to embrace the difficulties of missionary service, we need to assess whether God has given us the "grace" to endure these difficulties cheerfully. Has God given us the strength to look past these sufferings to our eternal reward, or will they distract us from Christ and lead us into temptation or despair?
- Missionaries should not choose difficult fields or ministries simply because of the difficulty. To the extent a prospective path might be unusually difficult for us, the difficulty itself may be only one factor in our ultimate decision, but it should generally incline us away from moving forward.
- Certain sufferings are "baked in" to the missionary vocation. We must be ready to endure these difficulties for years or decades. Furthermore, we should beware of missions methods that claim to create strong churches with shortened timelines or easier paths.
- We are easily overwhelmed by suffering, so when we pass through difficult seasons, we must pray for deliverance.

- As we wait for God's help, we should encourage ourselves with the reminder that God is faithful to deliver us. We should also seek out others to encourage us as well.

I realize that some of my readers may be going through seasons of suffering right now. If you are, I am painfully aware that there is nothing I can do through the pages of a book to ease your distress. Perhaps you've clung to the promises of Scripture and sought encouragement from the church, and your strength is still failing. And even if I could be there with you to grasp your hand, pray with you, listen to you, and maybe even weep with you, it would not take the edge off your pain. I can't offer you encouragement in the modern sense of the word—I can't make you feel any better or make your path any easier. But I perhaps can offer encouragement in the old-fashioned sense of the word—perhaps I can breathe courage into you in the midst of your suffering. Despite your pain—and even despair—God is with you. He will have the final word. And on the day when he does speak, it will be a word of redemption, reward, and healing.

6

Discipling Persecuted Believers and Churches

Jesus Christ did not say, "Go into the world and tell the world that it is quite right." The Gospel is something completely different. In fact, it is directly opposed to the world.

C. S. LEWIS
God in the Dock

GOD'S HOLY PRESENCE in our midst is what separates the church from the world. Paul writes:

> What portion does a believer share with an unbeliever? What agreement has the temple of God with idols? For we are the temple of the living God; as God said,
>
> "I will make my dwelling among them and walk among
> them,
> and I will be their God,

> and they shall be my people.
> Therefore go out from their midst,
> and be separate from them." (2 Cor. 6:15–17)

Paul quotes two Old Testament passages (Ex. 29:45; Lev. 26:12) to describe God's presence among his people, and he applies these passages to call the church to be separate from the world. He knows we face the same struggles Israel did as we follow God out of slavery toward his promised land. It's not easy to learn to dwell in God's presence, nor is it easy to learn how to be free. The Israelites wanted idols they could see (Ex. 32:1), which caused them to fondly misremember their experience of slavery (Ex. 16:3; Num. 11:4–5).

Sadly, Israel regularly failed to keep God's command to be separate from the nations. They succumbed to temptation and followed the ways of their neighboring nations. They worshiped idols and intermingled with the inhabitants of the land in ways that God prohibited. Ultimately, Israel's failure to separate herself from the world led her to lose her inheritance in the promised land (2 Kings 17:6–20; 24:10–17; 25:1–21).

Every church—whether on the mission field or not—should learn from Israel's mistakes. How can missionaries in unreached areas prepare churches to remain in the world while also being separate from it?

Before we go on, it may be helpful to mention that this chapter roughly follows the themes of the previous chapter. But rather than apply them to missionaries, I apply them to new believers and churches under their care.

A Case Study

I'd like to begin with a story to illustrate the importance of teaching believers in persecuted contexts how to deal well with persecution.

Not long ago, the team I serve on met a young man whom I will call Yusuf. Yusuf had confessed Christ after members of a nearby tribe shared the gospel with him. He had been baptized and had traveled to a nearby country to attend a six-month discipleship program whose mission was to raise up Christian leaders. Yusuf's friends and family, however, didn't know that he believed in Christ. Yusuf would sometimes join his Muslim friends when they lined up for prayer, but he would recite the Lord's Prayer in his heart. He lied to his friends and family about the discipleship program he attended, telling them he was traveling for work. Yusuf said that he intends to tell people the truth someday, but that he's waiting until there's a critical mass of believers to stand beside him.

Long-term missionaries in Yusuf's life don't see any of this as a serious problem. The director of the discipleship program that Yusuf attended has endorsed him as a mature believer. Like Yusuf, the missionaries hope that if a critical mass of people eventually comes to Christ, they will find strength to stand together.

It's critical to note how differently missionaries from the past would have responded to this situation. For example, some young believers once came to Adoniram Judson, requesting to be baptized. Judson wrote, "They appear to have experienced divine grace; but we advised them, as they had so little love to Christ as not to dare to die for his cause, to wait and reconsider the matter."[1] Judson made no attempt to pressure these believers to endure persecution and death if they weren't ready. He simply informed them that being ready to do so was an unavoidable part of following Christ.

We must not miss the implication of Judson's suggestion: Denying these young men baptism signified that he was not yet certain

1 Vance Christie, *Adoniram Judson: Devoted for Life* (Christian Focus, 2013), chap. 16, Kindle.

whether their faith was genuine. While Yusuf has received accolades from the missionaries in his life, Judson would have gently confronted his lack of faith. Rather than training Yusuf to be a leader, Judson would have seen his lack of readiness to confess Christ as a sign that he may not yet know Christ. What explains the different responses?

Avoiding Unnecessary Suffering

In order to answer this question, we first need to explore how today's missions community has come to view suffering. Thankfully, the wider missions community hasn't rejected the historical understanding that God can use suffering in redemptive ways. For example, missiologist Rebecca Lewis writes, "Persecution itself seems to weed out casual believers and keep churches vibrant."[2] Her position is widely accepted. Others have said:

> Overt persecution authenticates the faith within resistant cultures. Overt persecution gives faith value in the eyes of those who watch believers and marvel at their willingness to suffer and die in Jesus's name.[3]

> The movement with which we're connected has matured through the persecution believers are experiencing.[4]

While I'm grateful that the wider missions community remembers that God is faithful to work through suffering and persecution,

2 Rebecca Lewis, "Strategizing for Church Planting Movements in the Muslim World: Informal Reviews of Rodney Stark's *The Rise of Christianity* and David Garrison's *Church Planting Movements*," *International Journal of Frontier Missiology* 21, no. 2 (2004): 75.

3 Nik Ripken, "Recapturing the Role of Suffering," *Mission Frontiers* 32, no. 1 (2010): 6–9.

4 Andy Walker, "Advancing Through Persecution in North India," *Mission Frontiers* 41, no. 3 (2019): 28–29.

I'm concerned that many of us tend to speak about suffering only in positive terms. We speak of persecution as if it promotes church growth and maturation by default or as if it may provide ideal circumstances in which churches can thrive. In doing so, we largely ignore what the New Testament writers knew: Suffering and persecution are fearsome evils that Satan uses to attack the church (1 Pet. 5:8–9). If we fail to appreciate this truth, we can easily fall into a sort of triumphalism—not the sort that assumes persecution will always be easy to face but a subtler sort that speaks of persecution and its sufferings as a positive good for the church rather than an evil that God sometimes uses for the church's good. Like the children of Israel, if we fail to remember how weighty the hardships are that lie ahead, our courage may fail when we see just how powerful the giants in the land really are. As we continue, I will explain both why we need to avoid this sort of triumphalism and how it relates to Yusuf's story.

Protecting the Flock

First, however, let's examine how the Scriptures encourage us both to take persecution seriously and to avoid triumphalism.

Missionaries love Tertullian's comment that "the blood of the martyrs is seed" for the church.[5] The quote is scripturally sound, as far as it goes, and it recalls Jesus's statement that "unless a grain of wheat falls into the earth and dies, it remains alone; but if it dies, it bears much fruit" (John 12:24). But this quote is often used to suggest that persecution creates ideal situations for church

5 The popularized version of this quote from the early theologian Tertullian's *Apologeticus* has been somewhat poorly translated into English—it refers to the Neronian persecution and is better rendered "they sowed the seed of Christian blood" (Tertullian, *Tertullian: Apology. De Spectaculis,* trans. T. R. Glover [William Heinemann, 1931], 115)—but its meaning ultimately comes across.

growth. While Jesus confirms that God sometimes works through his people's sufferings to grow the church, he doesn't say that all persecution will always result in church growth. Yes, the church grew in persecuted China. But persecution essentially eliminated the church when Islam spread across the Middle East, North Africa, and South Asia. Similarly, the church has not grown in North Korea as it has in South Korea, or in India in the same way it has in Nepal.[6] Jezebel's persecution whittled down the remnant of Israel to seven thousand people (1 Kings 18:4; 19:18). In Acts 8:1–4, though persecution resulted in the church spreading beyond Jerusalem, it also seemed to end the church's burgeoning growth in Jerusalem. So while God can choose to work through persecution, Scripture doesn't suggest that it creates an ideal situation for church growth.

On multiple occasions, I've heard a missionary tell another Christian not to pray for persecution to end. Such statements seem bold and radical, but we should remember that the New Testament church prayed against persecution. For example, the church prayed for Peter's release in Acts 12, and Paul even told Timothy that prayer should be offered "for kings and all who are in high positions, that we may lead a peaceful and quiet life, godly and dignified in every way. This is good, and it is pleasing in the sight of God our Savior, who desires all people to be saved and to come to the knowledge of the truth" (1 Tim. 2:2–4). When Paul thought of situations that promote church growth—that led people "to be saved and to come to the knowledge of the truth"—he thought of situations that encouraged rulers to allow the church to live peaceably and quietly.

6 See Center for the Study of Global Christianity, *Christianity in Its Global Context, 1970–2020: Society, Religion, and Mission* (Gordon-Conwell Theological Seminary, 2013), 36, 38.

Additionally, as we saw in the previous chapter, Jesus himself told his apostles to flee persecution (Matt. 10:23). Jesus's concern for their safety is even clearer in Luke's account: "And he said to them, 'When I sent you out with no moneybag or knapsack or sandals, did you lack anything?' They said, 'Nothing.' He said to them, 'But now let the one who has a moneybag take it, and likewise a knapsack. And let the one who has no sword sell his cloak and buy one'" (Luke 22:35–36).

As Jesus indicates, these instructions are a reversal of the ministry pattern he gave when he initially sent out the disciples as missionaries (Luke 9:3; 10:4). With the danger of his crucifixion imminent, Jesus is temporarily releasing his disciples from their ministry obligations and telling them to do what they can to preserve their physical safety. John also notes Jesus's concern for his disciples' safety when he writes, "So he asked them again, 'Whom do you seek?' And they said, 'Jesus of Nazareth.' Jesus answered, 'I told you that I am he. So, if you seek me, let these men go.' This was to fulfill the word that he had spoken: 'Of those whom you gave me I have lost not one'" (John 18:7–9). We must display a similar concern for persecuted believers under our care. Certainly, if God calls them to suffer, then he will work through their suffering and even their deaths. But this is no reason not to protect them from suffering when we can.

I want to insist as emphatically as I can that once persecution becomes intense, it's not appropriate for church growth to be our primary ministry focus. Rather, our primary focus should be on getting people through persecution with their faith intact and—to whatever extent we can—with their minds and bodies intact as well. There are greater goods than the numerical growth of the church, and we must seek people's basic welfare even if that means that our ministries will absorb a substantial loss as we release them to flee to safety.

Even in the West, where persecution is less serious, we have seen scandals shake the church when pastors prioritize church growth over the well-being of vulnerable church members. In persecuted areas, the cost of giving in to such temptations may be far higher. Persecution can break people—it can traumatize and maim, bereave and martyr. So rather than seeing persecution as an ideal situation in which to minister, we should pray for it to end. We should do what we can to protect new believers from it and should support ministries that lobby wisely against it.[7]

Of course, Christ and his disciples don't "flee to the next" town every time people get angry with them. Instead, they do so when their lives are clearly in danger, when persecution interferes with their ability to minister, or when their presence becomes a cause of civil unrest (e.g., Luke 4:29–30; John 8:59; Acts 8:1–4; 9:23–25; 12:17; 13:50; 14:19–20; 17:13–15; 19:21–20:21). As his followers, we should normally flee persecution if there is credible danger to life or limb, unless there are overriding reasons not to.

To be clear, overriding reasons not to flee may exist. At times, not fleeing may provide opportunities to minister to others who are suffering or who are weak in their faith such that risking violence is worthwhile. In such situations, there is freedom in Christ. Those who choose to stay may do so, but any decision to stay should be made slowly and wisely.

7 If we understand the dark spiritual agendas behind persecution, we'll appreciate that political lobbying is likely very limited in what it can accomplish. Nevertheless, we should allow it to serve what purposes it can. After all, Paul used his political status as a Roman citizen to lobby against being mistreated on more than one occasion (e.g., Acts 16:37–40; 22:25–29), though it was not enough for him to avoid substantial prison time or, ultimately, martyrdom.

Here are some of the factors we must carefully weigh when we consider whether to stay or flee from persecution:

- whether remaining may put others in danger or aggravate the situation in ways that interfere with ministry that could be done (e.g., Acts 14:19–20; 17:13–15; 19:21–20:21)
- whether others who are in less danger can minister instead (e.g., 17:13–14)
- whether temporarily fleeing might allow for better opportunities to minister later on (e.g., 14:19–21)

Whenever we risk life or limb—perhaps by sending soldiers on a dangerous mission or by choosing to have a risky surgery—the outcomes remain in God's hands. We can't know if we'll achieve our goals or suffer loss along the way. But if we choose to endure life-threatening persecution, then we need to know that we have taken the risk as seriously as Jesus's instructions demand. We should not run toward persecution foolishly, but should be willing to flee until good reasons require us to stay.

Of course, new believers fleeing persecution won't usually mean emigrating to build a prosperous life in the West. In most situations, that won't even be possible. Instead, fleeing persecution means getting out of the way of danger until the danger has abated, as Christians did during Rome's persecutions. Peter fled Jerusalem when Herod wanted to kill him (12:17). But once Herod died (12:20–23), Peter returned (15:7). Early church leaders also followed this pattern. For example, Cyprian fled Carthage during the first Decian persecution (AD 250–251) and returned when it ended.

Today, believers can generally seek to withdraw temporarily if the threat of persecution arises. Nearer is better, so safety should first be sought in different neighborhoods or different cities rather than different countries or different continents. If that isn't possible, and if there is a way to flee the country, then a persecuted Algerian, for example, might consider fleeing to Tunisia before Dubai. But Dubai might be better than London or Atlanta.

Notably, in the New Testament, it is usually church leaders—Jesus,[8] Peter, and Paul—who flee persecution while their followers do not. As missionaries, we may feel uncomfortable when church leaders we have appointed flee and leave their flocks. When we're in danger, we may feel unsure about when we can leave those we're ministering to. Shouldn't we love them enough to die for them? Is it cowardly for church leaders or missionaries to flee?

As far back as the Roman Empire, persecutions have targeted church leaders with what seems to be a cruel sort of logic: "Strike the shepherd, and the sheep will be scattered" (Mark 14:27). Generally speaking, church leaders will find themselves in greater danger than other believers. In situations like these, when the danger is great, it's usually best for leaders to flee and allow others to minister in their absence. As Jesus told his apostles, "When they persecute you in one town, flee to the next" (Matt. 10:23).

Jesus's apostles took his encouragement to heart. Paul, for example, fled Lystra after he was stoned by angry crowds (Acts 14:19–23). He fled other cities when riots occurred in response to his preaching or when attempts were made on his life. He was not deserting the believers in Lystra, nor should we imagine that he was unwilling to suffer with his flock (Col. 1:24). Rather, Paul's

8 Of course, Jesus ultimately goes to the cross, but before doing so, he withdraws from persecution on numerous occasions (e.g., Matt. 12:14–15; Luke 4:29–30; John 8:59; 10:39).

departures seemed to keep his flocks safe because the riotous opposition evaporated when he left. This both allowed for others to minister in his stead (e.g., Acts 17:14) and for Paul to return shortly after opposition died down (e.g., 14:21).

Again, early church leaders were driven by a similar logic. When Cyprian fled the Decian persecution, his enemies accused him of cowardice. But he responded by noting his fear of what would happen if he stayed: "By my over-bold presence, the tumult which had begun might be still further provoked."[9] Leaving allowed him to return when the persecution subsided. We can take his statement at face value since he later proved that he was ready to die for his faith when the time came.

Our Curious Fear of Extraction

Thankfully, today's missions literature—both popular and academic—does not advocate seeking out persecution. But much of it still assumes that believers should never flee, and it seems to imply that if they are forced to flee, then something has gone wrong.

For example, Nik Ripken, perhaps the best-known Christian author today whose work focuses primarily on suffering and persecution, tells believers, "Do not run from persecution—and decide not to seek it."[10] He continues, "Decide not to extract

9 Cyprian of Carthage, "Epistle XIV," trans. Robert Ernest Wallis, in *Ante-Nicene Christian Library: Translations of the Writings of the Fathers Down to A.D. 325*, vol. 8, ed. Alexander Roberts and James Donaldson (T&T Clark, 1882), 49.

10 Nik Ripken, "Recapturing the Role of Suffering," 9. It may be helpful to note that despite Ripken's apparently hard line, he writes with genuine understanding and tenderness about people he has met who have fled persecution. For example, he tells of a woman named Samira who had "been forced to flee her country," writing with admiration rather than criticizing her choice to flee. See Nik Ripken, *The Insanity of God: A True Story of Faith Resurrected* (B&H, 2013), 319. Thus, any nuance missing in his writing may be present in his actual life and ministry. Nevertheless, I want to insist on nuance in our formal teachings. If it is missing,

a believer. Decide not to rescue others from sharing in the sufferings of Christ."[11] In his article "Should We Help Believers Escape Persecution?," Ripken never suggests that we should sometimes help our persecuted brothers and sisters "flee to the next town." Instead, he writes, "For God, conquering through persecution, rather than extracting from persecution, is the norm."[12]

Ripken explains that when we become "emotionally connected" to believers who are being persecuted, we help them escape. As a result, "the birth of the church is halted; in other places, the multiplication of the body of Christ is hindered. New followers of Jesus . . . come to believe that living in a safe, Christian country is necessary in order to live for Christ."[13] He even suggests that if the Western church gave "as much energy and attention to spreading the gospel in hostile places as we have to extracting persecuted believers from them, the Great Commission may have already been finished by now."[14]

I deeply appreciate Ripken's insistence that God is strong enough to sustain the church in times of persecution. Overall, his work has made an irreplaceable contribution to Western Christians' understanding of the gravity and prevalence of persecution throughout the world. Nevertheless, I'm concerned that his emphasis here could point us in directions that are—quite literally—dangerous. In his article, Ripken never acknowledges that the normal pattern of Jesus and his apostles was to withdraw when persecution became

---

then the missionaries we teach and the persecuted believers we advise may be left without a fully formed range of scriptural ideas as they decide how to respond to persecution.

11 Ripken, "Recapturing the Role of Suffering," 9.

12 Nik Ripken, "Should We Help Believers Escape Persecution?," Nik Ripken Ministries, August 23, 2016, https://www.nikripken.com/.

13 Ripken, "Escape Persecution."

14 Ripken, "Escape Persecution."

severe and that the gospel still spread. Ripken implies that we must choose between spreading the gospel and helping persecuted believers escape, and there appears to be no middle ground. In fact, if we extract a persecuted believer, Ripkin implies that we may have delayed the completion of the Great Commission. This latter suggestion is especially troubling because it places a needlessly heavy burden on believers who are already suffering.

We need to push back against teachings like these. For all their well-intentioned boldness, they miss the Bible's more careful treatment of the topic. In God's gracious sovereignty, we can trust that we will not—because we cannot—undermine the Great Commission by helping Christians follow Jesus's instructions to flee persecution. After all, the believers in Damascus who saved Paul's life by lowering him out of the city in a basket made an unparalleled contribution to the fulfillment of the Great Commission (see Acts 9:23–25). We can trust that God will advance the Great Commission through our efforts if we exercise wisdom when we counsel or help others to flee persecution.

The narrow range of choices that Ripken's article seems to consider—teaching people not to flee persecution or transplanting them to "a safe, Christian country"—are not the only paths we should consider. Other alternatives also exist that don't require transcontinental travel. We might consider relocating persecuted believers to a safe place in the area where they live, a safer area of the same country, or anywhere they can avoid persecution from authorities or family members. Often, the believers I have seen escape persecution simply went to stay with other believers until an abusive family cooled down.

And yet while not as common, there are times to help believers flee across international borders. Afghani pastors Ramazan and

Rahmat describe how they fled Afghanistan when the Taliban took over in 2021.[15] Because they had publicly acknowledged their faith, they were in great danger when the Taliban entered Kabul. They had only fifteen minutes to leave their homes, and they were in hiding for the next thirty-six days, constantly changing locations and often lacking food or a change of clothes. Pastor Josh Manley and his wife, Jenny, worked to arrange Ramazan and Rahmat's travel to the United States. Are we really in a place to decide that it would have been better for them to choose to stay or for the Manleys to leave them for the Taliban?

Not long ago, my wife and I were asked to help a young woman whose extended family had forcibly abducted her and had taken her away from her husband and child when they discovered that she and her husband were believers. We helped her escape and reunite with her husband and child. She even had to cross into a neighboring country to get out of her extended family's reach! Such stories aren't the everyday experience of most believers in persecuted areas, but they do happen, and we must take them into account.

Ultimately, Ripken's counsel risks missing how practical we must be in showing Jesus's compassion. For clarity's sake, let's imagine what we might do in a comparable situation in pastoral ministry. Suppose you are a pastor, and a woman in your congregation says that her unsaved husband is beating her. Would you encourage her to continue suffering, reasoning that Christ will be glorified as she shares the gospel with her husband despite his abuse? Or would you find safe housing for her as you minister to her and her family?

15 Jonathan Leeman, host, *9Marks Pastors Talk*, podcast, episode 217, "On Pastoring in Afghanistan, with Josh Manley and Two Afghan Pastors," 9Marks, November 8, 2022, https://www.9marks.org/.

In recent years, prominent Christian leaders have been forced to step down from their positions for choosing the first option, and we instinctively recognize its cruelty. We shouldn't imagine ministry overseas to be any different. Missionaries, like pastors everywhere, must actively seek the safety of those they minister to. This is a fundamental part of pastoring people well.

Nevertheless, the idea that new believers should not flee persecution is widespread. This is most clearly seen in the distinction many missionaries make between persecution and extraction. Persecution is most often discussed positively—even reverently to some extent. Extraction is a phenomenon Ripken warns against and that is nearly always discussed negatively in missions literature.[16] It is briefly defined as the withdrawal or expulsion of a new believer from his community of origin because of his faith in Christ. It is widely assumed that persecution will result in a growing church with a stronger witness, whereas extraction will weaken new believers and undermine their witness. For example, Rebecca Lewis suggests that extraction weakens the church: "The new aggregate church of extracted believers is rarely able to either provide the community support thereby lost or to continue to spread the gospel through its members' families, who now perceive the 'church' as having 'stolen' their relative or friend."[17] Brian Peterson agrees, noting that "the key issue at hand is whether or not new followers of Christ should be allowed to develop as disciples within the context of their own birth communities, whether Hindu, Muslim, Sikh, etc., or rather be extracted out of this social setting into

16 As noted above, "For God, conquering through persecution, rather than extracting from persecution, is the norm." Ripken, "Escape Persecution."

17 Rebecca Lewis, "Promoting Movements to Christ Within Natural Communities," *International Journal of Frontier Missiology* 24, no. 2 (2007): 75–76.

a more exclusively 'Christian' sub-culture."[18] Robby Butler says, "Extraction evangelism typically draws the marginalized from several peoples and segments of society—the elderly, youth, orphans, mission helpers and ardent seekers. The result is often a foreign, conglomerate church, alienated from the local peoples."[19] Lewis worries that extraction imposes a "Western paradigm of church formation based on Western individualism."[20] Others echo this concern, but is there any reason for us to accept this assumption?

The New Testament seems to show a very different pattern. A great deal of the persecution that the early church endured involved people being extracted from their communities—not because foreign cultures were being imposed on new believers but simply because their families, neighbors, or local authorities were angry that they were following Christ. Consider the following examples:

- The blind man Jesus healed was cast out of the synagogue (John 9:34).
- The Jerusalem believers were scattered (Acts 8:1).
- Paul escaped Damascus in a basket, running for his life (Acts 9:25).
- Paul was extracted from his community when he was imprisoned (Acts 21–28).
- The early readers of Hebrews were imprisoned (Heb. 10:32–34; 13:3).
- Timothy was imprisoned (Heb. 13:23).

18 Brian K. Peterson, "The Possibility of a 'Hindu Christ-Follower,'" *International Journal of Frontier Missiology* 24, no. 2 (2007): 87.

19 Robby Butler, "Indigenous Movements: How Peoples Are Reached," *Mission Frontiers* 40, no. 2 (2018): 8.

20 Lewis, "Promoting Movements to Christ," 75.

- Hebrews says, "Go to him outside the camp and bear the reproach he endured" (Heb. 13:13).
- Jesus warned his disciples, "They will put you out of the synagogues" (John 16:2), and he also said, "I have come to set a man against his father, and a daughter against her mother, and a daughter-in-law against her mother-in-law. And a person's enemies will be those of his own household" (Matt. 10:35–36).

The Scriptures don't distinguish between persecution and extraction, but they do speak of extracted believers with the same honor they extend to persecuted believers (e.g., Heb. 13:3). Indeed, it's hard to imagine how groups of believers could be persecuted by their communities in any serious way without some of them being extracted.

Do you see what's happened? When we underestimate the ferocity of persecution, we risk assuming that we must have done something wrong when new believers are driven out of their communities.

It's worth asking if our focus on explosive church growth has driven us toward these assumptions. Lewis warns that extraction may stop the gospel from spreading further, and her concern is broadly shared. H. L. Richard cites extraction as a reason why "there is no present effectiveness in winning Hindus and Muslims, so that attempts at new strategies are mandatory."[21] Other missions writers despair of extraction's effects on church growth. David Watson and Paul Watson argue, "Families perceive their loved ones as being

21 H. L. Richard, "Is Extraction Evangelism Still the Way to Go? Several Other Models Suggest Some Possible Alternatives in Mission to Hindus and Muslims," *Mission Frontiers* 18, no. 5 (1996), 14.

stolen or kidnapped from them. . . . And nations rarely tolerate traitors. Extraction churches are very difficult to reproduce."[22] Butler says, "Extraction evangelism makes peoples more resistant. . . . Extraction evangelism into conglomerate congregations actually hinders indigenous movements."[23]

We can't afford to miss the emphasis here. These discussions focus not on the spiritual and physical safety of extracted believers but on the missionaries' jeopardized ministry. I'm not implying that these authors don't care about persecuted people's safety. I'm sure they do. Nevertheless, advising so strongly against extraction because it imperils church growth risks leading missionaries to overemphasize numerical growth at the expense of persecuted believers well-being.

Church growth and extraction aren't mutually exclusive options. Remember, the church grew in Acts 8 after Christians followed Jesus's own instructions and fled persecution. Of course, we can't assume that God will always act in the same way. But whatever happens, we know that protecting our persecuted brothers and sisters from suffering won't interfere with God's good purposes.

What Should Believers in Persecuted Areas Be Ready to Suffer?

When extraction is characterized as a result of Western impulses that thwart church growth, then behaviors resulting in extraction will be labeled as "Western" and eliminated. By normalizing a suspicion of extraction, missionaries unintentionally communicate that the church can always thrive even amid terrible persecution. The fallout from such ideas is entirely predictable. New believers may

22 David Watson and Paul Watson, *Contagious Disciple-Making: Leading Others on a Journey of Discovery* (Thomas Nelson, 2014), 108.

23 Butler, "Indigenous Movements," 8.

feel pressure to expose themselves unnecessarily to imprisonment, abuse, or even martyrdom.

More common, however, is the temptation to make concessions to persecutors. If we see extraction as a sign that something has gone wrong, many of us will wonder whether new churches should adjust their theology and practices to avoid being expelled from their communities. Thus, ignoring Jesus's instruction to flee persecution can lead to ignoring Paul's command to flee idolatry (1 Cor. 10:14). By encouraging believers to avoid extraction from their communities, the missions community might have unintentionally incentivized patterns in which believers in Christ fail to separate clearly from the world. What began as a brave "whistling in the dark" can lead to compromise and syncretism.

At its extreme, this results in a set of missiological practices described as insider-movement methodologies. Insider-movement proponents have suggested that new believers should have freedom to "retain their identity as members of their socio-religious [communities]" and continue partaking in those communities' spiritual practices.[24] Believers from a Muslim background, for example, would continue to describe themselves as "Muslims" and pray at the mosque. They would bow with their neighbors during Muslim prayers while praying in their hearts in Jesus's name, much like Yusuf, whose story I told at the beginning of this chapter. We can safely assume he was influenced by insider-movement teaching and did not come up with this idea on his own.[25]

24 Rebecca Lewis, "Insider Movements: Honoring God-Given Identity and Community," *International Journal of Frontier Missiology* 26, no. 1 (2009): 16.

25 Gary Corwin notes how proponents of insider movements have commonly endorsed this practice. See Gary Corwin, "A Humble Appeal to C5/Insider Movement Muslim Ministry Advocates to Consider Ten Questions," *International Journal of Frontier Missiology* 24, no. 1 (2007): 5–20.

Proponents of insider movements justify such actions by arguing that a new Christian cannot renounce his religious community while maintaining a meaningful connection to his culture. Therefore, if we are truly to become "all things to all people" (1 Cor. 9:22), then all religious identities—along with their forms of religious expression—must be allowed within Christ's global church.

These assumptions have now been refuted in detail.[26] As missiologist Elliot Clark points out, 1 Corinthians 9:22 must be read in its larger context.[27] In 1 Corinthians 8–10, Paul is responding to a question from the Corinthians about whether they can eat meat that has been offered to idols. Paul says that they shouldn't, not because they aren't free to eat whatever food God has created (1 Cor. 10:19), but because Gentile believers may see what they are doing as practicing idolatry and be emboldened to return to idolatrous practices. Paul notes that "some, through former association with idols, eat food as really offered to an idol." He wants to guard against this weak person being destroyed, "the brother for whom Christ died" (1 Cor. 8:7–11). For Paul, being "all things to all people" doesn't mean eating food sacrificed to idols to avoid offending Gentile religious and cultural sensitivities; rather, it means drawing sharp boundaries to exclude certain Gentile religious and cultural practices so that Gentile believers won't be deceived into worshiping both idols and Christ (1 Cor. 8:10; 10:20). Paul warns that confusion on this matter could lead Gentiles not only into sin

26 See Joshua Lingel, Jeffery J. Morton, and Bill Nikides, *Chrislam: How Missionaries Are Promoting an Islamized Gospel* (i2 Ministries, 2012). See also Timothy C. Tennent, "Followers of Jesus (Isa) in Islamic Mosques: A Closer Examination of C-5 'High Spectrum' Contextualization," *International Journal of Frontier Missiology* 23, no. 3 (2006).

27 Elliot Clark, *Mission Affirmed: Recovering the Missionary Motivation of Paul* (Crossway, 2022), 173.

but also to destruction (1 Cor. 8:11). In the same way, Paul would have us "be all things to all people" by drawing sharp boundaries around Muslim, Hindu, or other worship practices lest we lead our brothers to stumble (1 Cor. 9:13). They need to see in us that they can't follow Christ without separating from their old beliefs and practices.

Clear boundaries between the church and the world don't exclude people from following Christ, as insider-movements practitioners suggest.[28] Instead, as Clark explains, "The dividing wall between Jew and Gentile is demolished (Eph. 2:14), but there yet remains a distinct boundary around God's holy temple."[29] We set boundaries between the church and other religions to keep people of all cultures safe within God's family. In all this, Christ is honored; the dividing wall between Jew and Gentile is demolished because we are one body in Christ. And the boundary separating God's people from the world remains because we worship Christ alone: "You cannot drink the cup of the Lord and the cup of demons" (1 Cor. 10:21).

Historically, God's people have always rejected the idea that Christians can identify with other religions while worshiping the one true God in their hearts. Daniel and his friends simply refused to bow to the golden image (Dan. 3:16–18; 6:10). Cyprian, the bishop of Carthage, was martyred under the Emperor Valerian for refusing to participate in "Roman rites."[30] Before he died, he forbade anyone from participating in any "sacrifice to idols . . . [in] the marketplace," and mourned those who chose

28 Indeed, Lewis goes so far as to suggest that "the nature of the gospel itself is at stake" if missionaries exclude Muslims or Hindu-background believers by asking them to renounce their previous religious identities. Lewis, "Honoring God-Given Identity," 17.

29 Clark, *Mission Affirmed*, 165.

30 W. H. C. Frend, *The Rise of Christianity* (Fortress, 1984), 319.

otherwise.[31] When the Reformation saints faced persecution, John Calvin condemned taking part in rites they did not believe in as "Nicodemism."[32] Peter Martyr Vermigli writes, "Satan would above all lead us to believe that we may serve God with our hearts even though we go through external rites and practice what is contrary to devotion. . . . This, surely, is nothing less than trying to convince us to serve two masters."[33] Throughout history, Christians have recognized that they cannot participate in religious rites they do not believe in or pretend to belong to religious systems they do not adhere to.

Today, too, believers must break allegiance with the religious systems of the world around them. There is no way to remain faithful to Christ while maintaining old allegiances. Thus, in our efforts to contextualize the gospel, we must not focus exclusively—as today's missions literature tends to do—on removing unnecessary cultural barriers that stop people from believing in Christ. Certainly, that's an essential part of contextualization and clear communication. But on its own, it's not enough. Faithful contextualization also involves finding culturally appropriate ways to preserve the differences that exist between Christ's people and the world.

This doesn't mean people like Yusuf always have to advertise their identity as believers in Christ. Sometimes Christ himself

31 Cyprian of Carthage, "De Lapsis," trans. Robert Ernest Wallis in *Ante-Nicene Christian Library: Translations of the Writings of the Fathers Down to A.D. 325*, vol. 8, ed. Alexander Roberts and James Donaldson (T&T Clark, 1882), 354. Cyprian writes, "I need tears rather than words to express the sorrow with which the wound of our body should be bewailed."

32 John Calvin, *Excuse à Messieurs les Nicodémites* (1544). In using the term "Nicodemism," Calvin criticizes people who pretend to take part in religious rites they don't believe in by comparing them to Nicodemus, who, in John 3, knew that Jesus was sent from God but came to Jesus by night to hide his beliefs from his contemporaries.

33 "Prefatory Letter," in *Trattato della vera chiesa catholica*, trans. Mariano Di Gangi, quoted in *The Peter Martyr Library*, vol. 1 (Thomas Jefferson University Press, 1994), 22–23.

chooses not to advertise aspects of his identity (e.g., Matt. 21:27). But there is nothing secretive about his ministry and message. On the contrary, he begins his ministry with a messianic claim (Luke 4:16–19), does miracles in public, teaches crowds of thousands, openly denounces the religious authorities (Matt. 5:20), and says things like "I am the bread of life" (John 6:35). Jesus does decline some opportunities to acknowledge his Messiahship directly (e.g., Matt. 21:27), but he generally does so when his enemies attempt to entice him into making statements that they can use against him and his ministry.[34]

In the same way, persecuted believers should feel freedom not to proactively advertise their belief in Christ to those with evil intentions. There are times for wise and appropriate nontransparency. Nevertheless, our lives should be characterized more generally by a desire to proclaim the truth of Jesus and his message. Persecuted believers should avoid crossing lines of deceit and, unlike Yusuf, should not participate in religious rituals they don't agree with. They should be careful that wise nontransparency doesn't deteriorate into a general posture of hiding their faith in Christ. John writes that some of the religious leaders in Jesus's day believed in him but "they did not confess it, so that they would not be put out of the synagogue; for they loved the glory that comes from man more than the glory that comes from God" (John 12:42–43). John's comment reminds us that while there's a real difference between dishonesty and nontransparency, it may not always be enough just to avoid lying. Instead, believers should also avoid any murkiness about their faith that's motivated by a desire to avoid rejection.

34 It's worth noting that Jesus does acknowledge his Messiahship in answer to the chief priests' question (Matt. 21:33–44) but he does so in a parable, rather than in a single, easy-to-understand statement that they could use to easily attack him.

Fortunately, the influence of insider movements has somewhat abated. But they have left behind a widespread tolerance for believers living their Christian lives in secret, even if it means lying about their belief in Christ. Too often, people aren't taught that a fundamental part of believing in Christ is trusting that the reward he promises is worth any persecution one might endure. The missionaries closely involved with Yusuf don't see his deceptiveness as a problem in his life or as a mark of immaturity. Their hope that Yusuf might avoid extraction from his community by delaying obedience to what Christ commands unintentionally prioritizes ministry growth over his spiritual maturity. But it sabotages any hope of real ministry growth. The missionaries around Yusuf have joined with him in hoping that a large number of believers may eventually grow around him so that he can confess Christ more easily, but they fail to see that he is only contributing to an increasing number of people who listen to Christ's teaching but don't feel that it's necessary to confess him as Lord.

We must work against these trends, teaching people as early as possible in our evangelism that God is calling them to a fundamentally different life. Explaining to people how God calls them out of the world can act as a filter by separating those with Spirit-filled hearts from those with fear-filled hearts. We can be clear about the difficulties of following Jesus while still being gentle, respectful, and welcoming. Jesus is kind, gracious, and patient, but he still calls people to repent or face certain destruction. Peter not only welcomes the crowd at Pentecost to believe in Jesus, but he also warns them to save themselves "from this crooked generation" (Acts 2:40). Paul's sermon in Athens is respectful and even compliments the Athenians as "very religious" (Acts 17:22), but he pulls no punches in calling them to leave their idolatry or face judgment (Acts 17:29–31).

In contrast, many missionaries today are largely taught to avoid controversy. They tell the gospel story in ways that minimize differences and share stories about Jesus's power and kindness to avoid correcting the false teachings of surrounding religions. These actions are well-meaning but fail to recognize that people will naturally find ways to incorporate the parts of Jesus's teaching they like into their non-Christian worldviews and lifestyles. Too often, they end up treating Jesus's teachings as just one more facet of the truth. In Jesus's day, the scribes and Pharisees diminished God's law by incorporating it into their lives in ways that still allowed them to pursue their fleshly impulses (Matt. 5:17–48). If we do not clearly call new believers out of the world, we leave them susceptible to a similar temptation. If Jesus's way isn't different, then few people will see any reason to take his message seriously.

Many evangelism strategies condense sharing the gospel into a presentation of Christ's death and resurrection on our behalf. But it may not be enough to explain how Christ's death is necessary to save us if we don't explain his divinity to Muslims or his exclusivity to Hindus and Buddhists. For example, modern missions methods often neglect to mention Christ's divinity to Muslims in the process of evangelism. And it's not unusual for his divinity to be largely glossed over through follow-up discipleship programs that are designed to help new believers plant new churches. Similarly, despite the prevalence of idol worship in Hinduism, modern missions methods often neglect to mention the exclusive claims of Christ to Hindus before declaring them evangelized and sending them out to share the gospel with others.

Why are such basic gospel presentations marketed as sufficient? Their designers are certainly wonderful Christians who have the best of intentions, and I don't question their orthodoxy or sincerity. Perhaps they assume that anyone who accepts Christ's death has now given their heart to Christ and will fall under the Spirit's conviction as other key points of doctrine are revealed. Yet if so, why not reveal these points up front?

Supposed new believers evangelized through such methods may continue to believe that Christ is a lesser prophet than Muhammad or that he is simply one of many gurus or enlightened teachers or gods to be worshiped. They may have admitted that their works are insufficient to save them, but they may see believing in Christ's death for them as simply one more prerequisite of salvation or enlightenment. They may still fast during Ramadan and pray Muslim prayers five times a day, or they may continue to practice Hindu or Buddhist rites. Crucially, these "new believers" may not understand that part of following Christ is embracing convictions that require leaving their previous religious communities behind. They may never have counted the cost of doing so. While they may be sent to share the gospel, their witness and message are uncompelling and insufficient. A message that can fit into cultural beliefs people have always held has little to offer them that is unique, urgent, or ultimately true. Therefore, we should explain from the beginning of our evangelism that the Christian message goes against much of what they have believed and practiced.

Where I live and work, Muslims often make statements like "Islam and Christianity have so much in common." As a new missionary, I would respond by affirming some of the beliefs that do overlap, hoping to establish common ground. Now, after many years on the field, I've learned that it's far more important to explain our differences. I now respond, "Yes, they certainly do share some things in common, but the differences between them are far more significant." Jesus himself began his preaching not by emphasizing how similar the gospel was to people's prevailing worldview but by telling them they needed to "repent, for the kingdom of heaven is at hand" (Matt. 4:17). From the beginning, Jesus assured them that the righteousness of the Pharisees and scribes—the prevailing religious system of the day—was useless for entering the kingdom of heaven (Matt. 5:20).

I understand how well-meaning missionaries fall into such mistakes. Perhaps they lack theological training, or perhaps, in their eagerness for fruit, they soften difficult aspects of discipleship. But such an approach ultimately puts real victory at risk.

If we downplay the ways Christ's teachings differ from other religious systems and assume that the church will always continue to grow numerically, despite persecution, we open the church up to a variety of dangers. These can include:

- a lack of emphasis on repentance as a part of conversion
- false conversions
- premature affirmation of people's faith
- a lower standard of discipleship that does not call believers to carry the cross like Jesus did
- the affirming of immature believers as mature and appointing them to leadership
- a minimizing of doctrinal differences between Christianity and other world religions
- blending Christian teachings and spiritual practices with teachings and spiritual practices that the New Testament denies or forbids (i.e., syncretism)

As I write this, I am praying for Yusuf. We don't know yet whether he is the type of seed that responds enthusiastically to Jesus but falls away when persecution comes or the type that remains steadfast and bears fruit (Matt. 13:18–21). If he were to share his faith, his life would not easily proclaim a Christ worth living and dying for. His message might not offend people, but it might also not have anything compelling to offer them.

Teaching People to Face Persecution

We have no choice but to insist that it's impossible to follow Christ without being different from the unbelieving communities around us, even if doing so results in persecution. Certainly, we should allow new believers to flee severe persecution when necessary. But when fleeing is unnecessary or impossible, how do we prepare them to endure persecution?

We can begin by praying for new believers and sharing biblical insights with them. We must teach a robust theology of suffering, persecution, and hope. This book means to contribute to that conversation. Let me offer a few thoughts about sharing what we've already covered with Christians who face persecution.

First, we should remember that in areas where a wider local church exists, persecuted believers should never suffer alone. We saw in the previous chapter how we can endure suffering only through God's strength, which comes to us, in part, through our brothers and sisters. That's why the author of Hebrews reminds his suffering readers to take encouragement from their leaders' example (Heb. 13:7) and insists that they offer encouragement to each other (Heb. 3:13; 10:24). Sin and disbelief can be tempting as we suffer for Christ, so the author says, "Take care, brothers, lest there be in any of you an evil, unbelieving heart, leading you to fall away from the living God. But exhort one another every day, as long as it is called 'today,' that none of you may be hardened by the deceitfulness of sin" (Heb. 3:12–13).

Notice it's the congregation whom he instructs to "take care" that no one in their midst falls into unbelief. They do so by exhorting each other (cf. Heb. 10:25). For the author of Hebrews, congregational encouragement helps individual believers survive. Later, he commends his readers for partnering with those who were persecuted and for visiting those who were imprisoned (Heb. 10:33–34). He instructs them to continue doing so (Heb. 13:3), which is a public and potentially dangerous step. Preparing new believers for persecution isn't simply a matter of teaching individuals to be ready to suffer. We also need to prepare the wider churches we plant or pastor to encourage each other in times of persecution. They need to be taught how to stand together, even if they suffer for doing so. When it is possible, churches should help believers decide how to respond to persecution. If they do flee, the churches should maintain contact with them until they return. Similarly, believers should be taught to look to their churches for wisdom, strength, and support. We're not made to function alone. "If one member [of the body] suffers, all suffer together" (1 Cor. 12:26).

Where my wife and I work, persecution intensifies during the month of Ramadan for believers who choose not to fast along with their friends and neighbors. Spending entire days together allows believers to eat and drink in a way that does not provoke their hungry and thirsty neighbors to envy or anger. The sense of togetherness they feel with each other strengthens them to bear the rejection they feel from their wider community.

Second, as we disciple new believers in persecuted areas, it's not helpful to push people to take risks or demonstrate levels of commitment to Christ they're not ready for. Jesus doesn't pressure his followers by telling them that since he came to lay his life down for them, they should be grateful enough to lay down their lives for him (though they should be). Instead, he explains that they will receive eternal life if—and only if—they deny themselves, take up their cross, and follow him (e.g., Luke 9:23–25). He knows that faith in the resurrection and the reward he offers can prepare people to obey in ways that obligation can't.

The New Testament writers echo Jesus's approach, emphasizing both the rewards of trusting Jesus enough to follow him through suffering and the consequences of failing to do so.[35] In the same way, we prepare people to face persecution by reminding them of the eternal rewards to be gained for trusting Jesus amid great sufferings and of the eternal losses if they don't. There are, of course, other motivations that can spur us to obey Christ (e.g., gratitude, the joy of being "counted worthy to suffer" [Acts 5:41], etc.), and we should make every effort to grasp as many of them as we can. But ultimately, these motivations won't last if we do not believe that God is going to keep his word and reward us. We can't seek first God's kingdom and his righteousness if we don't believe "all these things will be added" to us (Matt. 6:33). That's why, after insisting true faith believes that God "rewards those who seek him" (Heb. 11:6), the author of Hebrews explains that "by faith Abraham obeyed" (Heb. 11:8). Specifically, his faith in God's promise to grant him a future inheritance motivated him to leave his homeland (Heb. 11:9–10). He was even willing to offer up his promised son because he believed God would reward his obedience and raise Isaac from the dead (Heb. 11:17–19). Similarly, when the cost of

35 See Matt. 10:28, 39; Mark 8:35; John 12:25; Rom. 8:18; Heb. 12:1–2; 1 Pet. 4:12–13; Rev. 2:10.

obedience is high enough—when our lives or our children's lives are on the line—we will be able to obey only if we believe God will take care of us.

Third, we should be as clear as possible when preparing people for what might lie ahead. Jesus does this repeatedly in the Gospels (e.g., Matt. 10:17–39; John 16:1–2). He didn't want his disciples to be surprised when their families or religious communities rejected them, nor did he want them to be shocked when they encountered death threats. People hypothetically believe that obeying God is worthwhile even when difficult. Yet our perspectives change when our family rejects us, we lose our job, or we face the threat of being beaten or imprisoned. We're more capable of doublethink than we realize, and real struggles like these refine and test our faith more than abstract ideas do.

So whenever possible as we evangelize, we should speak concretely about suffering. Explain the situations believers may face and explore how Jesus's promises make these situations worthwhile. As Hebrews 11 points not only to the suffering of the saints but also to their reward, so our discipleship should as well.

Finally, many missionaries were raised in Christian families in countries with minimal persecution. It's easy to think that persecution will affect our disciples but not us, which leaves us feeling guilty about teaching new believers to suffer for Christ. Is it fair to ask them to endure what we haven't? Such sentiments are well-meaning but shortsighted. God may decree tomorrow that we must endure terrible persecution, or it may be cancer, bereavement, or unbearable pain. Even if he doesn't, no one benefits when we downplay the truth because we may not have to endure as much as others. Just as a doctor who has never endured cancer still needs to encourage a cancer patient to suffer through painful, life-saving therapy, we need to make Jesus's life-giving path clear, even when we haven't endured such forms of suffering ourselves.

Conclusion

Some readers will wonder if it's ever wise to encourage new believers to flee persecution. Am I being too easy on them? I hope what I have argued reflects Scripture's call to suffering believers, which is both easier and harder than the prevailing wisdom in missionary circles today. It's easier because Scripture sees suffering as a great evil and encourages us to avoid it when we can. It's harder because in many situations it can't be avoided, and Scripture calls us to be ready to suffer well. Scripture never tells us to appease our potential persecutors by downplaying our religious identity and allegiances. Missionaries must hold fast to these biblical emphases, even in the face of significant ministry losses.

What does this mean practically? In this chapter, we have seen that:

- When persecution becomes severe, our primary focus should be on helping people survive with their faith intact and—to whatever extent we can—with their minds and bodies intact as well.
- We must do what we can for their basic safety, even if that interferes with our hopes for church growth. We must be willing to counsel them to leave situations in which we hoped that they could minister.
- Fleeing persecution does not usually mean permanently relocating or moving across international borders. It often means going to stay with other believers until a dangerous situation cools down.

- We must not pressure people to take a stand for Christ when they are not ready. We must communicate what Jesus expects but be patient if it takes time for them to follow.
- We must care for the faith and integrity of persecuted believers, teaching them that Jesus expects them to renounce unscriptural religious practices and pre-Christian religious identities, no matter how angry their communities become or what short-term ministry losses may result.

When true transformation happens in the lives of even a few people, and when the hope of the resurrection sets them free from the fear of suffering and death, the beacon of their faith may topple empires. Of course, God doesn't guarantee such grand outcomes. What happens is in his hands. Even when churches show remarkable wisdom and integrity, persecutors sometimes win the day. But that's just the point. If we have moved beyond the fear of death to a bright hope in our future resurrection, we will be less concerned about winning the day and more concerned about God's eternal purposes. Altering or obscuring Christ's teachings about suffering may grow our numbers in the short term, but it will certainly strip our witness of its clarity and power. Let us be zealous for God's house (John 2:17) and do all we can to keep the church pure. God himself walks in our midst.

7

Poverty, Wealth, and the Missionary Calling

Wherein have we missed in setting before them
the wrong ideal that they should regard money
as of more worth to seek after than souls.

JIM ELLIOT
The Journals of Jim Elliot: Missionary, Martyr, Man of God

DURING THE REFUGEE CRISIS I described at the beginning of chapter 2, a group of young men approached my team and said they wanted to follow Jesus. Their entire tribe was Muslim, but they had previously lived in other refugee situations and had met missionaries and Christians from other tribes. This gave them a degree of familiarity with Christianity. We couldn't tell at first whether any of them understood the gospel, and we saw no signs that they were ready to take a difficult stand for Christ.

Still, it was a good beginning. We started a Bible study with them and had several lively discussions for the first few weeks. The study grew for a while but then fizzled out. Sometime later they asked us to start a Bible study again, and we did. This time, however, it lasted for only two weeks, and then they stopped coming. After the third or fourth false start, some of the more influential young men in this group approached us and explained that we were doing things the wrong way. They said we could easily reach hundreds of people if we helped them start an NGO (a nongovernmental organization that provides aid) that would give each of them jobs. They assured us that once this happened, other refugees would be interested in coming to hear more about Jesus.

NGO jobs are among the most lucrative forms of employment where we live. NGOs take considerable time and finances to run, and our team was both unable and, ultimately, uninterested in sponsoring this project. When that became clear, the group of young men evaporated.

A few weeks later, two of them contacted me. They told me that a missionary who had come through our town had convinced them and many of their friends to get baptized. I was surprised and wondered if they were ready, but their minds were made up. There was little time to talk about their decision, so I decided to do what I could to support them. The next day I watched as a handful of my friends were baptized by this eager missionary.

A few days later, however, the same two young men approached me, this time with intense concern on their faces. "Who is he?" they demanded.

"Who?" I asked, confused.

"This man who baptized us. Who is he? What church did he come from? What NGO is he with?"

"I don't know," I responded. "I didn't bring him here, and I wasn't here when he talked with you."

"Matt," they told me, "he promised people a lot of things. We need to know what church or NGO stands behind him. We need to know if he can do what he promised."

As we talked, they explained that the missionary had promised to take at least ten people back with him to the country he had flown in from. These men would then be discipled and trained. They would learn English, study the Bible, and have their room and board paid for, and then they could return to their people to work as pastors. They continued, "We're refugees, Matt, and we have nothing. Lots of people wanted to become Christians when he said that. And if he doesn't keep his promises, it will look very bad for Jesus. And it will look bad for us because we hosted the meeting where he promised these things."

Shortly after this, I ran into a young man whom this missionary had baptized and described as a "leader" in the group. When I asked if he understood why Christ had died, he looked at me blankly, confusion written on his face. He thought for a moment and then tentatively said, "Well, I guess he died because they crucified him." Well, that's technically correct. But this man had no deeper understanding of the reasons for Christ's death. When I spoke with him about Christ's deity, he was surprised and said, "In Islam we see him as a prophet." His use of the pronoun "we" stung because he still included himself in the fold of Islam. Though he had been baptized, he neither understood the basics of the gospel nor identified himself as a Christian. As I spoke with him, however, it became clear that he did hope strongly in at least one thing: a better life. Therefore, he wondered if this missionary might make good on his promise to give him one.

I'm not suggesting that this missionary meant to mislead these people with promises of material welfare. Perhaps he spoke about flying people to his country because he imagined they would need some sort of training if they were going to return and evangelize their people. Nevertheless, the missionary did not understand how such an opportunity might appeal to these people and lead them to make commitments they did not yet understand.

It's with stories like this one in mind that I wrote this chapter, hoping to especially address missionaries who serve in areas that are considerably poorer than their home countries. I want to encourage such missionaries to consider how their relative wealth may affect their ministries. The story above vividly illustrates a problem missionaries often face in subtler forms. We come offering the gospel, but the wealth and possible economic benefits we offer can incentivize people to listen to us for the wrong reasons.

God has always expected his people to leave the world and its treasures behind. For example, Abraham "went out, not knowing where he was going, . . . to live in the land of promise, as in a foreign land" (Heb. 11:8–9). When Moses led God's people through the wilderness, he left behind the luxuries of Egypt (Heb. 11:26), and the people left behind Egypt's provisions (Num. 11:5). Today God's call is not simply for us to leave our homes for a new land but for us to regard ourselves as "strangers and exiles on the earth" (Heb. 11:13). This is why the New Testament is so critical toward loving the riches of this world.[1] We must uproot ourselves from this present world and follow God, even though we cannot yet see the new life in which he has promised to establish and enrich us.

1 See e.g., Matt 8:19–20; 13:22; Luke 1:53; 6:24; 12:13–21, 33; 18:25; 2 Cor. 8:9; 1 Tim. 6:6–10; James 1:9–11; 2:5; 5:1; Rev. 18:19. Notably, there are no passages in the entire New Testament that portray earthly riches in a positive light, though there are a few that can be used to show that owning riches is not inherently sinful.

The New Testament does not oppose riches per se, but it certainly opposes putting our hope in the riches of this age. Instead, we ought to be concerned primarily with building up treasure in the next life, the life that endures. In fact, it's vital that we do so because pursuing riches for eternity is a sign that we trust God to lead us there. Abraham left Ur because he trusted God's promise to make him a great nation (Gen. 12:1–9). Moses left Egypt because he trusted that God could offer him a greater reward than the court of Pharaoh (Heb. 11:23–28). The point of Luke's parable of the dishonest manager (Luke 16:1–9) is that our days here are ending, so we should use the short time we have left to invest in the long future that lies ahead. We will happily give up treasures in this life to store up treasures in the next if we truly believe in God's promise to raise us from the dead and richly reward us.

It would be difficult to overstate how consistently negative the New Testament is about the "desire to be rich" (1 Tim. 6:9) in this world. Sometimes it uses language that is downright shocking, but we should not dismiss this language too quickly. Yes, Jesus was likely using hyperbole when he said that "it is easier for a camel to go through the eye of a needle than for a rich person to enter the kingdom of God" (Luke 18:25). But hyperbole still communicates something, and we can't afford to ignore Jesus's lesson. The desire to store riches in this life as opposed to the next is a sign of spiritual rot.

You may wonder why I'm talking about money in a book about the role of suffering and persecution in missions. But the temptations of wealth and persecution are dangerous in the same way. As the temptation of persecution uses our fears of suffering in this world to blind us to the realities of the next, so the temptation of wealth uses our desires for pleasure and security in this world to blind us to the realities of the next. Both temptations offer an escape from suffering.

The sad popularity of prosperity gospels preached around the world reveals just how alluring the promises of pleasure and security in the world can be. And the two temptations often work hand in hand. One of the first things persecutors often do is seize our money or try to impoverish us (see Heb. 10:34; Rev. 13:7). Part of the suffering God calls faithful people to in this world is to focus primarily on storing up treasures in heaven even though our lives would be easier if we focused on storing up treasures here and now (see Matt. 6:19–21; 1 Tim. 6:9; Heb. 11:24–26).

New Testament Missionary Poverty

What does this all mean? Should those of us who have high-paying jobs quit them? Should we stop trying to invest wisely? Should we swear off all worldly wealth and live in monasteries? I don't think so.

The New Testament may discourage us from storing up treasure in this world, but it doesn't idealize poverty. Poverty, like all suffering, is an evil in this world. The New Testament commands people on multiple occasions to help the poor (e.g., Matt. 19:21; 25:35; Gal. 2:10). Moreover, we know that the early church made a practice of supporting widows (Acts 6:1). Paul insists strongly on the responsibility of believers to provide financially for their families (1 Tim. 5:4), condemning anyone who doesn't as "worse than an unbeliever" (1 Tim. 5:8). He summarizes:

> For we brought nothing into the world, and we cannot take anything out of the world. But if we have food and clothing, with these we will be content. But those who desire to be rich fall into

> temptation, into a snare, into many senseless and harmful desires that plunge people into ruin and destruction. (1 Tim. 6:7–9)

A New Testament view of money encourages us to invest our lives and fortunes primarily in eternal things. At the same time, it insists that part of doing so is to provide for our own families' basic needs in this life while being sensitive to, and interested in, meeting the needs of the poor around us.

Here's a quick thought experiment that might help illustrate what this looks like. Suppose you found an investment opportunity and had some way to be certain that after a few years, any money you had invested in it would grow exponentially. What would you do? If you had the resources, you'd probably budget enough money to stay out of poverty for the next few years. But beyond that, you'd probably shift as much of your spending as you could—and maybe even tighten your belt some—to take advantage of this opportunity in any way possible. That's how Christians are meant to live regarding eternity. We should not aim to impoverish ourselves or our families, but at the same time, we should be strongly motivated to make all our economic decisions in light of the exponential gains—far beyond our wildest dreams—that we'll soon receive if we invest in the next life now. The point isn't to embrace poverty in this world but to invest this world's wealth in pursuing eternal riches.

And yet, though poverty is not idealized more generally, Jesus places special economic restrictions on the missionaries he sends out. He tells his apostles, "Heal the sick, raise the dead, cleanse lepers, cast out demons. You received without paying; give without pay. Acquire no gold or silver or copper for your belts, no bag for your journey, or two tunics or sandals or a staff" (Matt. 10:8–10; cf. Luke 9:1–5). He gives similar instructions to the seventy-two (Luke 10:4–9).

Many people will point out that Jesus's instructions here weren't given to us but to the twelve apostles and that most missionaries today can't follow them literally. I agree. I certainly haven't been able to heal the sick or raise the dead! But while Jesus's instructions to the apostles and the seventy-two were not spoken to us directly, they are still written—like the rest of Scripture—for our instruction (see 2 Tim. 3:16–17). In fact, the pattern set here is consistent throughout the New Testament. Missionaries in the New Testament never once deviate from relating to money according to the pattern Jesus gave to the apostles and the seventy-two. Consider these examples:

- Jesus himself chooses to minister from a place of poverty, though he could have easily acquired wealth or even been made a king (John 6:15).
- Peter's response to the beggar in the temple recalls Jesus's earlier injunction to the apostles not to carry money: "I have no silver and gold, but what I do have I give to you. In the name of Jesus Christ of Nazareth, rise up and walk!" (Acts 3:6; cf. Luke 9:1–5).
- Paul describes himself as "poor" (2 Cor. 6:10) and says of himself and Barnabas, "To the present hour we hunger and thirst, we are poorly dressed and buffeted and homeless, and we labor, working with our own hands" (1 Cor. 4:11–12).

Notice the pattern of how Jesus, Peter, and Paul did their missionary work. They didn't travel into an area promising wealth or displaying the signs of wealth, like a missionary promising to fly people back to his country or give them jobs with an NGO. If anything, their own finances were fairly meager: "I have no silver and gold," said Peter. Why might they have followed this pattern when they could have worked in other ways?

It's worth noting that before Jesus's arrest, when he knows his disciples will be in hiding and unable to minister, he releases them from the financial constraints they need to follow while ministering: "Let the one who has a moneybag take it" (Luke 22:36). The economic restrictions New Testament missionaries follow, then, are meant to be followed only for the duration of their ministries and are given for the sake of their ministries. But why? We could easily think they would have been able to minister more effectively if they had carried gold and silver and used them to help the people they were sent to serve. But Jesus knew how easily "the cares of the world and the deceitfulness of riches choke the word" (Matt. 13:22), and how quickly this can trick us into imagining that we can "serve God and money" (Matt. 6:24). He also knew how naturally people imagine "that godliness is a means of gain" (1 Tim. 6:5), and how this deception saddles them with "harmful desires that plunge people into ruin" (1 Tim. 6:9). So the meager lifestyle that was modeled by Jesus and other New Testament missionaries was intended to protect people from such double-mindedness. By being "poor" in this age, they hoped to make "many rich" in the next (2 Cor. 6:10; cf. 8:9). This was important enough to Jesus that he challenged some would-be disciples to be ready to endure periods of homelessness if they wanted to follow him (Matt. 8:19–20). Jesus and other New Testament missionaries were working in a society where poverty was widespread. Like all missionary sufferings, the economic restrictions they embraced served as a spectacle—a theater—for the gospel to be enacted in front of people so that they might believe (1 Cor. 4:9). As God provided for his missionaries and empowered their ministry to succeed despite their meager resources, the people they served witnessed firsthand how real and substantial God's riches are and how fleeting and deceptive the wealth of this age really is.

Missionary Wealth Today

And here we missionaries often find ourselves conflicted. A large portion of our missions force is sent from nations with highly developed economies, and we are often sent to poverty-stricken nations. We don't want to violate Jesus's instructions, but we wonder, "Doesn't God want us to use our financial resources to benefit those we serve?" We not only want to speak a message of eternal salvation but also want to act to deliver people from the suffering of this world. Former International Mission Board president Jerry Rankin writes:

> Mission history has been replete with an unfortunate tension between evangelism and social ministry. Obviously, there have been those who have sought to proclaim the life-transforming message of the gospel while ignoring the suffering and physical needs of their listeners. Likewise, there have been those who confined their witness to the good works they might do while never offering the recipients spiritual hope.[2]

To Rankin, this is an issue of integrity. For many missionaries, it's also a key to success: People are too smart to be taken in by the hypocrisy of words without actions. How will they believe our

2 Jerry Rankin, foreword to *Preach and Heal: A Biblical Model for Missions*, by Charles Fielding (International Mission Board, 2006), Kindle.

message of eternal salvation if we preach it while ignoring their tangible needs?

Many proponents of *holistic mission* take similar ideas a step further. They argue that if we truly want to provide people with holistic deliverance, then we must work to meet their holistic needs. This involves not only helping individuals who are suffering through medical or dental needs, for example, but also transforming their society since individual wholeness cannot be reliably maintained amid a broken society. Such transformation, they claim, is impossible without lifting people out the economic and social systems that have left them impoverished. Thus, the Lausanne World Conference for Evangelization's Issue Group on Holistic Mission states:

> The pursuit of justice for the poor is not the whole of holistic mission but it is a key component. For example, there are many aspects of the discussion about how wealth is produced and distributed in economics, but from the biblical perspective, the bottom line is how any economic system impacts the life of the poor. Biblically, justice is defined by the inclusivity of the God who defends the cause of the orphan, widow and immigrant.[3]

Quite frankly, we missionaries often feel the example of New Testament missionaries—which we examined above—and the desire to bring economic deliverance to those we serve pulling us in two opposite directions. Nuance is needed, so follow me closely.

The wider church should certainly promote human thriving and should work toward societal healing where it can. Nevertheless, while Jesus and other New Testament missionaries often healed

3 *Holistic Mission*, Lausanne occasional paper no. 33 (Lausanne Committee for World Evangelization, 2004), 9, https://lausanne.org/.

people through the power of the Spirit, they never worked directly to bring economic prosperity to a society—or even to select individuals—as a part of their ministry. Jesus could have chosen not only to teach the gospel but also to introduce people to the principles of modern marketing, education, manufacturing, or democracy. I suspect this would have alleviated some of their suffering. He could have let the people make him king (John 6:15) and could have then worked against injustice, poverty, and oppression. But he refused. He turned away from worldly methods of helping people and the worldly means it would take to implement them. Rather than giving his disciples an economic advantage, he made it clear to them that following him would mean a life of economic hardship. While it is true that people come to Jesus with mixed motives throughout the Gospels, it's also true that he proactively corrects the motives of those who come to him seeking financial success (Luke 12:13–21).

Moreover, Jesus not only prohibits the missionaries he sends out from ministering through financial means but additionally sends them out dependent on the communities they are to serve. He says:

> Carry no moneybag, no knapsack, no sandals. . . . Whatever house you enter, . . . remain in the same house, eating and drinking what they provide, for the laborer deserves his wages. . . . Whenever you enter a town and they receive you, eat what is set before you. Heal the sick in it. (Luke 10:4–9)

To the extent that New Testament missionaries minister to people's tangible needs, they do so entirely by the supernatural power of the Holy Spirit. In fact, the people they minister to are supposed to contribute to their needs by hosting them. Only Paul and Barnabas refuse to take any support from the churches they plant (1 Cor. 9:4–11). In this, they see themselves as unique, and they certainly don't bring material blessing to their churches. Rather, Paul asks the Gentile churches under his care to return money to the church in Jerusalem (Rom. 15:26–27).

Ministry Platforms

Missionaries today can follow similar patterns. Even when they are sent from affluent countries to poorer countries, they should expect the message of the gospel to have its own authority. They need not take "gold or silver or copper for [their] belts" (Matt. 10:9) in order for their message to be compelling. Certainly, there are some countries that missionaries cannot access without large NGO grants or business platforms. But the financial reach of these programs cannot add to the credibility or power of the gospel. Rather, it may prove to be a significant liability to the gospel by confusing listeners' motives.

Missiologist Elliot Clark recalls speaking with a young missionary who described encountering difficulties in his early years on the field:

> He happily volunteered the solution he had discovered. With the help of some locals, he was operating a non-governmental organization (NGO) that worked on community development projects throughout the region. He was grateful to report how this platform supplied him with legitimacy, served the needs of struggling communities, and provided access for the gospel in unreached areas. It sounded perfect. Villages were gladly opening their doors to the work of his NGO, which ultimately opened the door for the gospel. "It's amazing," he added, "the

> opportunities you have for evangelism when you bring $50,000 worth of investment into a local community."
>
> I was suddenly bewildered. Perhaps he sensed the surprise and confusion on my face, because he went on to explain further.
>
> Recently he'd had the opportunity to meet with a municipal official in a remote region, someone he assumed would otherwise never hear the gospel or at least have an interest in listening to it. But since this missionary's NGO was investing heavily in his village, the official was more than happy to give him his undivided attention.[4]

Do you see the danger here? Jesus taught that we cannot serve God and money (Matt. 6:24), yet this well-meaning missionary was entirely unaware of the mixed message that occurs when you dangle this world's riches in front of people to bring them to Jesus. Nor was he aware of how the financial desires kindled by doing so might compete with a desire to know Christ. Perhaps it's possible to cobble together a sort of "church" out of people who come to Jesus with financial motives, but it would not be possible to do so without the danger that many might prove unfruitful, like seed sown among thorns (Matt. 13:22). Lasting fruit is unlikely to result from apparent ministry successes that come from the power encounter of our wealth with others' poverty, rather than from the weakness encounter of the cross meeting the power of the world.

Patronage Systems

I'm sure every missionary today would shudder at the idea of buying converts or of spreading a prosperity gospel outright. Yet we

4 Elliot Clark, *Mission Affirmed: Recovering the Missionary Motivation of Paul* (Crossway, 2022), 40.

can unknowingly fall into a similar trap if we fail to understand how different cultures interact with money. In order to avoid this trap, we need to understand how easily people in poorer countries can see missionaries as significant financial patrons—as tickets to financial success—without the missionaries realizing it.

SIL missionary Harriet Hill comments, "Stepping off the plane in Africa, we should be greeted by large posters saying, 'Welcome to the land of patron-client systems.' It would help us all to get along better."[5] Essentially, patronage is a long-term reciprocal relationship between the "haves" and "have-nots." It's particularly common in societies where widespread poverty forces people into interdependent relationships. The haves benefit the have-nots with their money and influence, while the have-nots reciprocate by acting as a helpful entourage that serves and honors the haves. Patronage is common not only in many African countries, as Hill notes, but also in nations across the world that remain economically underdeveloped.

People in these societies do not see patronage as unusual or surprising. One author reflects:

> Such inequality is not a problem to be solved; it is a fundamental part of how the world works. . . . Friendships are made with this in mind. Local people do not need classes in how to practice patronage; it is a part of their understanding of life. Patronage thinking resides in subconscious attitudes. . . . Interdependence is seen as desirable, in addition to being necessary. Any person who seeks to be autonomous is morally suspect.[6]

5 Harriet Hill, quoted in Colin Bearup, *Clues to Africa, Islam, and the Gospel: Insights for New Workers* (William Carey, 2020), 99.

6 Bearup, *Clues to Africa*, 100.

Missionaries from wealthy societies struggle to understand how deeply patronage affects their friendships. In wealthy societies, responsible individuals can usually find ways to be economically self-reliant, so it's widely expected that trustworthy people shouldn't use their friendships for financial gain. However, in societies where poverty is endemic and economic self-reliance is often impossible, the assumption is the opposite: Trustworthy people shouldn't withhold money from their friends. Thus, when missionaries from wealthy countries go to serve in poorer countries, it's almost impossible for them to understand how their wealth affects their relationships with the people around them. This is especially the case for missionaries who have an NGO or other lucrative business platform. But even if we don't have such platforms and job opportunities, we may still establish ourselves as patrons by giving irregular gifts or loans that are significantly larger than local people would receive from their friends, family members, or neighbors.

There's nothing morally wrong with patronage systems. The New Testament authors never speak against them even though they seem to have been a common feature of New Testament society. The elders in Capernaum repay the centurion's patronage by asking Jesus to heal his servant (Luke 7:3–5). James is aware enough of the power of patronage to warn his readers not to pay any special deference to rich people in their congregations (James 2:1–7). At various points, people even appeal to Jesus for socioeconomic help. They either expect him to intervene through his personal influence ("Teacher, tell my brother to divide the inheritance with me," Luke 12:13), or through the wealth and power he will acquire as Messiah ("Say that these two sons of mine are to sit, one at your right hand and one at your left, in your kingdom," Matt. 20:21). After Jesus feeds the five thousand—addressing a fundamental economic need in a hand-to-mouth, agrarian society—people try to make him king (John 6:15).

Although patronage is not morally wrong, Jesus never acts as anyone's financial patron, and he doesn't help people climb the economic ladder. The apostles and other New Testament missionaries follow his example, even drawing strong distinctions between the gifts they can give and those they refuse to give: "I have no silver and gold, but what I do have I give to you. In the name of Jesus Christ of Nazareth, rise up and walk!" (Acts 3:6). The New Testament missionary community repeatedly affirms that people must pursue economic success independent of their involvement in the church (2 Thess. 3:10; 1 Tim. 6:5). Certainly, the church does what it can to make sure its widows don't starve (Acts 6:1–6), but New Testament saints are far more likely to be impoverished than enriched for following Jesus (Heb. 10:34). Missionaries today should also do what we can to avoid becoming patrons to those we serve.

Avoiding Financial Patronage

This can be harder than we imagine. There are occasions when financial patronage is unavoidable. Missionaries may need to hire language tutors or find themselves working in countries where entry is impossible without a business or NGO platform. Friends or neighbors may have medical emergencies so severe that they are likely to die if we don't give a large gift—the kind that will mark us, ever afterward, as their patrons in their minds. These may not be optimal situations for discipleship and evangelism.

Nevertheless, ideal situations are rare, and wisdom often requires us to do the best we can with what we have. If you find yourself unable to avoid patronage, then you should do what you can to be fair and generous. Keep salaries commensurate with what your employees would earn if they weren't working for you. If you must employ people, then a salary that doesn't rocket them to previously unknown levels of prosperity may allow them to appreciate you as an employer without seeing you as their ticket to financial success.

Nevertheless, while certain patronage situations may be unavoidable, we must push against these tendencies where we can. Refusing people's requests for patronage can be heart-wrenching. For example, imagine that a friend comes to you, and you know that his children have been wearing old clothes the past few months. You have spent real time with this friend and developed a deep affection for him. He's been working hard—you've seen it—to acquire the venture capital to start a small store. Then his brother is badly injured in a car accident. As medical costs pile up, your friend's savings vanish. So he asks for help. For only a few hundred dollars, which he earnestly promises to repay, you might be able to help turn his life around. Perhaps you've done this for one or two friends already and you know how wonderful it will feel to lend him the money. You've already experienced the grateful tears, embraces, and repeated blessings: "May God give you twin boys! May God put you in a special place in heaven!" Even if you do it only once, such a gift will certainly establish you as a patron. But you trust your friend enough that you don't imagine your generosity could have any real negative effects on such a close friendship. And anyway, isn't this exactly what Jesus would want us to do?

If you hope to minister to your friend as a missionary, then the answer is probably not. While you are free to help your friend, you should probably offer a smaller gift, of the size given by friends rather than patrons. After all, Jesus had all of God's wealth available to him, but he didn't deal in large business loans, and neither did early New Testament missionaries. Jesus consistently emphasized to his disciples that they would suffer economic loss in this world if they followed him. That was okay because they would gain riches in the next (e.g., Matt. 6:19–21; 8:20; 19:21; Luke 12:13–21; 16:9, 19–31). He refused to minister by bringing prosperity to people in this world because he knew that doing so would distract them from coming to him to seek eternal life and treasure in the next world.

Again, I'm not suggesting that Jesus's wider church shouldn't try to help people find good jobs or address issues of systemic economic injustice. It should do so in whatever way is possible. I am, however, suggesting that when missionaries first enter an unreached community to preach the gospel, it's counterproductive to take on these roles. So then, how do missionaries actually live among poor people without becoming their patrons? How can we do so while honoring Jesus's commands to care for the poor?

First, we need to live largely at the level of the people we have come to serve. We should have similar housing, similar food, similar clothing, and similar methods of transportation. It may be helpful to note that, in most societies, people's economic circumstances vary widely. In the town where my wife and I live, some people struggle to afford donkeys while others have cars. There is a range of economic levels we can live at while still ministering to people who will not be overly distracted by our wealth. Nevertheless, the higher we live on the economic scale, the more people will find our wealth a dangerous distraction.

The missions community tends to assume that the standards of living people can endure are more or less hardwired into them. Thus, a missionary family might end up embracing economic practices that are obviously ostentatious, but the wider missionary community (mistakenly) tells itself that no harm will come, especially if they are still enduring far harder living conditions than they would in their countries of origin.

It's not my place to act as a financial conscience for other believers. It's not morally wrong for missionaries to live at an economic level higher than that of the people they are sent to reach. Yet we would do well to reflect on the issue more. Missionaries to poverty-stricken areas should be taught before leaving that, where possible, living at similar levels to their neighbors may be an important part of their ministry. Can they endure such difficulty? We must remember that our lives are a theater, so where poverty is widespread, it may be vital to demonstrate the sufficiency of Christ's power and joy amid poverty.

Of course, missionaries shouldn't see living meagerly as a righteous end in and of itself. Missionaries who are parents should do what they can to provide their children with a strong family culture that includes ties with their country of origin. This will usually require owning books, educational materials, media, and keepsakes from home. But these can be kept in private spaces. After all, mementos from our home cultures may be confusing to our local friends and neighbors if they communicate a noticeably higher standard of living.

It's worth noting that Christ himself did not continue to rely on his carpentry skills to supply his economic needs. He accepted gifts to finance his ministry rather than rely on a trade (Luke 8:3). Perhaps in a similar way, occupying ourselves with the tasks poorer people around us occupy themselves with can interfere with our own ability to minister. In some societies, for example, computer technology might be virtually unheard of, but investing in it can cut years off the time it takes to learn languages and translate

Scripture.[7] Gas stoves or house helpers may seem extravagant to our neighbors, but they may also free up vital time for ministry. Similarly, we may need to buy a vehicle if our ministry requires us to travel frequently, even if most of our neighbors cannot afford one.

I can't give you definitive answers as to which purchases you should or shouldn't make. Wisdom is required because the specifics of each situation differ. For example, my wife and I resisted hiring local house help for years. But then we found ourselves raising two infants, and in between washing laundry by hand, making trips to the market, cooking, washing dishes, hosting, visiting neighbors, and caring for our family, there was no time left for anything else! We hired a house helper to take care of some of these tasks, and this bought us much-needed time for my wife to continue with language study.

Because there are no one-size-fits-all answers, missionaries should be taught to reason carefully through any purchases and lifestyle decisions that create obvious economic gulfs between them and their neighbors. Before leaving for the mission field, they should be ready to embrace the discomfort of economic hardship when it benefits their ministries, just as they should be ready to embrace the discomfort of long years away from their extended families.

Second, we should look for ways to practice generosity without becoming long-term patrons. Jesus and his apostles maintained

7 Most missionaries will learn languages far quicker if they are able to make good audio recordings of the language they are learning and study from these recordings. Computer technology can be used to make and organize recordings easily. Good translation software can help us, among other things, to compare passages for consistency, coordinate our translation choices with those of colleagues, check interpretations used by major Bible translations, research textual variants and usage of various scriptural terms in original languages, offer options for formatting, and help translation checkers.

a fund to help the poor (John 12:6), but they did not practice generosity in ways that left impoverished people viewing them as stepping stones to financial success. Missionaries whose ministries involve regularly serving the poor with considerable gifts or finances might consider maintaining a "gap" between their evangelistic work and the bulk of their giving. We can focus our giving to the poor on projects that don't directly benefit the people we are discipling but still show our investment in their community. For example, the team I work on has donated substantial resources to a local school. When people we are discipling ask us for larger gifts, we explain to them that much of our charitable giving has gone in this direction.

This approach is especially helpful in contexts where missionaries can gain visas only by developing a highly funded "entry platform." If you can gain access to your country of ministry only by founding an English school for children, an NGO, a lucrative (by local standards) restaurant, or another business, you will likely find that your efforts to disciple your employees are complicated by your economic position in their lives. However, you can additionally invest in evangelistic relationships with people who have no economic relationship to your business or NGO work.

Again, this doesn't mean we never give financial gifts to close friends or people we are discipling. In many cultures, the idea of keeping finances and friendship separate is hard for people to understand—if you love your friends, why wouldn't you share money with them when they have needs, or give to them at weddings, celebrations, and funerals? But we should generally try keep our gifts within the range that is normal for generous people in the societies we serve in.[8] This allows our gifts to show real generosity

8 There is a certain amount of subjectivity here. In most cultures, the size of an appropriate gift will be determined both by the occasion and by your closeness to the person receiving the gift.

without constituting a rung up on the economic ladder. It also leaves room for their families and wider communities to shoulder whatever portion of the giving that should appropriately fall to them. Similarly, the early church helped provide for widows to eat (Acts 6:1), since refusing to address this basic need could have been negligent. But it gave a "daily distribution" rather than providing larger handouts, and wherever possible, it demanded that widows' families provide for them instead (cf. 1 Tim. 5:3–7).

It's also possible to get creative. We can help the poor in simple, nonfinancial ways. One time a friend came to me and my wife complaining of a bad foot wound. My wife has some medical background, so she was glad to help. Over the course of a few weeks, she cleaned the wound, cut off dead skin, applied bandages, and ultimately taught him to care for it himself. The wound healed wonderfully, and not a cent changed hands.

Finally, a few readers may feel that in some cases, the economic gap between us and those we serve is simply too wide to reach across. I've often heard it argued that there is no real way for missionaries from wealthy countries to live at the economic level of their impoverished friends. I could give away every penny I own, for example, but if I were ill, I would still have a wealthy American family that could fly me home to hospitals that offer state-of-the-art medical care. If I were imprisoned unjustly, then I would still have citizenship in a powerful country that would probably intervene. My local friends have none of these resources. At times, it might be even immoral of me not to avail myself of them. For example, if one of my children had leukemia, then it would be wrong for me not to care for him to the best of my ability (e.g., 1 Tim. 5:8). I would spend everything I had to fly my child to a developed country to have the disease treated. If a similar situation occurred with one of my local friends' children, then the child would probably die.

All this is true, but the point is not to reach a level of poverty exactly equivalent to that of our friends. While I cannot get rid of the wealth and influence of my American friends and family, I can still share in people's experiences in meaningful ways. Jesus continued to have the resources and power of heaven itself at his disposal while on earth, yet for the duration of his ministry he still "became poor" for our sake (2 Cor. 8:9; cf. Phil. 2:6–7).

In the same way, even if we have resources at our disposal to acquire wealth, we can experience real poverty during our ministries. We can get the same sicknesses, travel the same broken-down roads, and live in the same corruption-ridden systems. Indeed, if our family connections, educational attainment, or nationality allow us certain opportunities, then we may also suffer in ways our neighbors do not by living at a distance from our families and home cultures. The point is not for us to achieve the exact level of economic hardship with everyone we meet, for no two people can suffer in the same ways. Instead, the point is to set aside the economic practices that inflame people's desire for wealth and make it harder for them to be attracted to the hope and joy of God that they see in us.

Conclusion

Years ago, an acquaintance of mine, who I'll call Heather, began sharing the gospel with a young man I'll call Daniel. He was deeply intrigued by the claims of Christ. He was also deeply intrigued by Heather, and the two of them began dating. If you had talked to Daniel at this time—and I did, at some length—he would have told you he was genuinely interested in Christ, and he would have maintained that his interest in Heather was an entirely separate matter. He was interested in Christ for the claims of Christ and in Heather for the attraction of Heather. I'm convinced that he sincerely believed this to be the case. Indeed, part of what made it so hard for Heather to break off their relationship was that she was convinced that, as she shared the gospel with him, her presence was helping—not hindering—his ability to make up his mind about Jesus. But eventually, she decided the relationship was not working and ended it.

Do you know what happened next? Daniel's interest in Christ immediately faded. While he had sincerely believed his interest in Christ was separate from his interest in Heather, the magic that made Jesus's claims urgent and attractive was closely linked to the magic that made his relationship with Heather urgent and attractive. When the magic of Heather ended, the magic of Jesus faded too, and a few weeks later, Daniel had nothing to say about the subject except that Christians were a bunch of hypocrites.

Do you see the problem? Some roles don't mix well. There's nothing wrong with singles dating other singles, and there's nothing wrong with evangelizing unbelievers. But it's not healthy to mix dating and evangelism. In the same way, there's nothing wrong with patronage, but it's not advisable to mix patronage and missionary service. Even in our home countries we wouldn't think it was ideal for a pastor to minister to a church largely made up of his own employees.

During my years on the mission field I've consistently been surprised by the power of patronage to corrupt otherwise healthy relationships between missionaries and locals. I've seen promising young leaders lie and exaggerate ministry successes, claiming they had led groups of people to Christ and started multiple Bible studies when they had not. I've seen otherwise earnest new believers lie about expenses or fabricate needs in order to take money from missionaries. I've seen national believers fight over whose right it was to benefit from the patronage of new missionaries. Missionaries can't afford to miss the danger they put new believers in by acting as their financial patrons.

Indeed, Daniel would have been less confused about his motives for inquiring about Jesus—and perhaps less likely to decide in the end that Christians were hypocrites—if Heather had not encouraged his interest in her. In the same way, it's not only unreached people but also missionaries whose fascination with money can lead to an unhealthy patronage.

As a missionary, I've sometimes found it harder than I imagined to lower my standard of living. I have offered inappropriate types of financial assistance when I wanted to help people through their present distresses and forgot the eternal distress that faces them. Like Heather, I didn't intend for relationships to turn unhealthy, but when they began to show signs of ill health, I was slow to realize that the relational patterns I was creating might render me more of a hindrance than a help to Jesus's work in people's lives.

How did this happen? Perhaps I was too caught up in the power of money and the benefits I derived from being a patron to see clearly. Every time people who are interested in Christ approach me for money, a part of me still thinks, "Just give it to them. How will they understand Christ's goodness if you send them away disappointed? Let them tangibly see the love and generosity of Christ's people at work." But then I must remember that the message we bring is far more valuable than any financial help we could offer. It is powerful enough to work entirely apart from financial incentives.

All those whose eyes and hearts are open to Christ's message will accept this.

My hope in this chapter is to help missionaries consider the poverty Jesus required of his own disciples in greater depth. As they do, they can keep these key takeaways in mind:

- The New Testament does not speak against riches, but it does speak strongly and consistently against storing them up in this world—indeed, storing up riches in this life rather than the next may indicate that we don't believe in Jesus's eternal life to come.
- Jesus and other New Testament missionaries embraced relative poverty while they ministered. They didn't want to tempt people to come to Jesus expecting earthly riches, and they warned those who listened to them that following Jesus might result in poverty in this world.
- Missionaries from affluent countries who minister in poverty-stricken areas should follow this New Testament pattern and do what they can to avoid becoming patrons.
- Missionaries should generally try to live at an economic level that is close to that of their neighbors.
- Missionaries may need to lay aside any economic practices that tempt people to equate following Jesus with economic success in this world.
- We need to believe that our message alone—unaided by any economic benefits—has the power to call people to leave everything behind and follow Jesus.

It's not always easy to believe that the gospel is powerful enough to call people to Jesus even if they don't benefit economically.

One of the strongest temptations I have experienced in ministry came during the story I told at the beginning of this chapter, when my local friends promised that a church would grow if my teammates and I helped them start an NGO. It felt like such a small compromise, and refusing their invitation didn't seem to make sense at all. Yet Jesus's call is clear. We must store up treasure in heaven, not on earth (Matt. 6:19–21), and must teach others to do the same. May we strive for the promised land God is leading us toward and put every hindrance aside. As we do, may we avoid putting any stock in the riches of this world, teaching those we disciple to do the same.

Conclusion

Soon we shall be in heaven. O let us live as we shall then wish we had done. Let us be humble, unaspiring, indifferent equally to worldly comfort and the applause of men, absorbed in Christ, the uncreated Fountain of all excellence and glory.

ADONIRAM JUDSON
The Life of Adoniram Judson

HOW DO WE REACH the vast regions of the world that remain unreached by the gospel? Although this question requires a multifaceted answer, Scripture suggests that an essential part of the answer is to address the challenges that suffering and persecution pose to the spread of the gospel. The fear of death has the same power today that it did two thousand years ago. It can still hold people in slavery (Heb. 2:15), and we see how effectively it continues to do so in the least-reached areas of the world.

It's not hard to understand why the fear of death is so powerful. People who don't have the certainty of a new, immortal life waiting for them must do everything they can to avoid death, postpone it, or perhaps even deny it will happen. All the while, the knowledge that death *is* coming seizes people with a desperation to squeeze what sweetness and meaning they can out of each stage of life.

But those who know Christ shouldn't live in such fear and desperation. Yes, death will come (Heb. 9:27). But for those of us who know Christ, death itself will be over swiftly, and we will enter a life infinitely longer and more joyful and substantial than our brief stay on this earth. God wants us to be an eternally minded people who look forward to that day. Through the slow todays and tomorrows of this world, we know a different day is coming when he will set everything right. Paul writes:

> The appointed time has grown very short. From now on, let those who have wives live as though they had none, and those who mourn as though they were not mourning, and those who rejoice as though they were not rejoicing, and those who buy as though they had no goods, and those who deal with the world as though they had no dealings with it. For the present form of this world is passing away. (1 Cor. 7:29–31)

The hope of eternal life will strengthen us to endure necessary suffering and loss as we follow Jesus toward the promised land. Of course, we should never take that suffering lightly. But no amount of pain or loss—or even death itself—will be able to turn us back from following Jesus if we have faith that God will reward us and redeem our sufferings.

As we wait for that day, we should call as many as we can to join us. Those of us who are gifted for missionary service will do so by ministering in places where the fear of suffering has blinded entire tribes and nations to the gospel. Our message must call people in these places to a hope of resurrection that enables them to throw off the chains of fear and stand amid a hostile and malicious world, unwavering and unmoved by its threats.

This is the patient hope that sustained the early church under three hundred years of Roman persecution. At its worst, Rome's persecution was harsher than anything we've seen in the modern world, featuring entire stadiums full of people who paid for the privilege of watching Christians get torn apart by wild animals. Yet Jesus's promise of eternal life and an eternal reward was enough to sustain his people through their terrible sufferings. Missionaries should strive to impart the same hope in people they reach today.

Polycarp, one of the last living disciples of the apostle John, had an effective ministry despite Rome's persecution. His Roman opponents called him "the overthrower of our gods, who teacheth many not to sacrifice or to worship."[1] He protected the churches that grew under his care, causing "many to turn away from the . . . heretics to the Church of God."[2] What missionary today would not be grateful to be commended with similar words?

When Polycarp became a target of Roman persecution, he followed Christ's instruction and fled. He was ultimately found, arrested, and brought into a Roman stadium. In front of a bloodthirsty crowd, the Roman proconsul asked him to renounce Christ. He responded, "Eighty-six years I have served him, and he never did me any wrong. How can I blaspheme my King who saved me?"[3] Polycarp knew that God had been good to him all along, and he knew that he could trust God to bring him safely to the

1 *The Church History of Eusebius*, trans. by Arthur Cushman McGiffert (Eerdmans, 2019), 180.

2 Eusebius, *Church History*, 180.

3 "The Martyrdom of Saint Polycarp," in *Early Christian Fathers*, ed. Cyril C. Richardson (Simon and Schuster, 1995), 152.

journey's end. So when the proconsul called for him to be burned alive, Polycarp looked up toward heaven and said:

> Lord God Almighty, the Father of thy beloved and blessed Servant Jesus Christ, through whom we have received full knowledge of thee, "the God of angels and powers and all creation" and of the whole race of the righteous who live in thy presence; I bless thee because thou hast deemed me worthy of this day and hour, to take my part in the number of the martyrs, in the cup of Christ for "resurrection to eternal life" of soul and body in the immortality of the Holy Spirit; among whom may I be received in thy presence this day as a rich and acceptable sacrifice. . . . I praise thee, I bless thee, I glorify thee, through the eternal and heavenly High Priest, Jesus Christ, thy beloved Servant, through whom be glory to thee with him and the Holy Spirit both now and unto the ages to come. Amen.[4]

The Roman Empire had mastered the art of cruel theater, and Polycarp's death served as a spectacle for the people of Rome. At its crudest and most basic level, it was simply the afternoon's entertainment, a spectacle of suffering for curious, adrenaline-seeking attendees who found a fleeting, bloodthirsty excitement in the horror of watching strangers die.

At a second level, one only slightly more sophisticated, Polycarp's death was an enactment of Roman power. Rome always made the suffering of her enemies public, and the message was clear: "Don't defy us—or this will happen to you."

4 "The Martyrdom of Polycarp," 154.

At a third level—one that was much darker and deeper, and that even Rome's cruel rulers were unaware of—Polycarp's death was an enactment of the despair that had taken hold of the world as its dark powers held men and women in slavery and asserted their dominance. The message here was one of sinister intimidation: "Look what happens to those who trust this Savior and his God to deliver them."

But at a fourth and final level, far deeper than all the others—one that only Polycarp and his friends were aware of—his death served as a message of hope, a reenactment of a redemptive story that would one day end the gladiator games and subvert the brutality of Rome itself. God's own power was on display in Polycarp's courage. A spectacle greater than even the spectacle of death itself caught the minds of some who were watching, so that they recorded his death for posterity. Even the bloodthirsty Roman crowd was not unmoved. Early church historian Eusebius quotes an ancient letter written after Polycarp's death. It was written by the church he presided over, and the letter tells us that Polycarp "put an end to the persecution, having, as it were, sealed it by his martyrdom."[5] The Roman crowds saw an old man so deeply convinced of God's goodness that he was ready to die. They saw a man who had already seen enough traces of the next world that the hope of its glory beckoned to him, even if he had to first endure a torturous death. And somehow, their bloodthirstiness waned, and the persecution fizzled out.

Polycarp was full of hope as he submitted himself to martyrdom. But those of us who trust in Christ know that at that moment his suffering journey ended and his sacrifice was accepted.

5 Eusebius, *Church History*, 177.

The practice run was over, and his real life had finally begun. This is the hope that we invite all people everywhere to embrace. This is the hope that spurs our own journey onward toward the promised land.

Acknowledgments

I BEGAN WRITING this book after Jonathan Leeman encouraged me to do so. He saw value in it in its earliest (and driest) stages, providing excellent editorial feedback to help me refine it. Alex Duke edited for style and content and helped make a good deal of jumbled, archaic-sounding text more readable. Don L. provided theological and editorial help with an early draft of this manuscript. His careful wisdom was a blessing to me, as it has been at various points in my adult life. My dad also provided theological and editorial help. His outlook on life and Scripture has enlightened and corrected my own—and continues to do so—in ways that I become more aware of each year.

My wife, Kim, read through this manuscript again and again and always responded with encouragement. She aided me in editing and refining the manuscript and has stood by me as we've wrestled with the sufferings we've encountered in our lives. She has helped me hold my head above water and continue trusting in God's goodness at many points when I have felt I was sinking. She has been a greater part of God's goodness to me in this life than she will ever know.

General Index

Scripture Index

Building Healthy Churches

9Marks exists to equip church leaders with a biblical vision and practical resources for displaying God's glory to the nations through healthy churches.

To that end, we want to see churches characterized by these nine marks of health:

1. Expositional Preaching
2. Gospel Doctrine
3. A Biblical Understanding of Conversion and Evangelism
4. Biblical Church Membership
5. Biblical Church Discipline
6. A Biblical Concern for Discipleship and Growth
7. Biblical Church Leadership
8. A Biblical Understanding of the Practice of Prayer
9. A Biblical Understanding and Practice of Missions

Also Available from Matt Rhodes

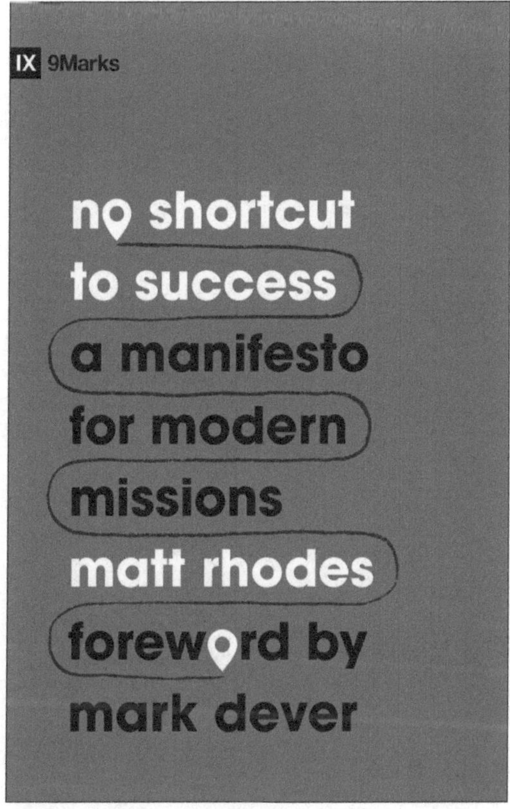

In *No Shortcut to Success*, author and missionary Matt Rhodes encourages Christians to stop chasing silver-bullet strategies for missions and embrace long-term methods grounded on theological education, clear communication, and a devotion to ministry excellence.

For more information, visit **crossway.org**.